The Learning Zone: Connecting Your Student's Heart, Mind, and Purpose

Book Two in Raising a Generation of Leaders

By
Tiffany Earl
and
Heidi Christianson

The Learning Zone: Connecting Your Student's Heart, Mind, and Purpose

Book Two in the Raising a Generation of Leaders Series

AI Assistance Statement:
This book was edited with the assistance of AI, which helped with structural organization, content refinement, and editorial suggestions. All final decisions about content, style, and presentation were made by the human authors and editors.

First Edition: March 2025

Library of Congress Control Number: [Number to be assigned]

ISBN: 979-8-9922395-0-8

Printed in the United States of America

For information about permission to reproduce selections from this book, contact: Genius Paradigm Publishing
info@realizinggenius.com

TABLE OF CONTENTS

CHAPTER 9

Writing: Developing Voice and Vision

CHAPTER 10

Tutorial: Facilitating Deeper Understanding
Through Collaborative Learning

CHAPTER 11

Coaching: Nurturing Growth
Through Personalized Guidance

CHAPTER 12

Lectures: Transforming Information into Inspiration

Table of Contents

ACKNOWLEDGMENTS

First and foremost, we want to acknowledge the co-founder of LEMI and contributor of many of the principles talked about in this book, Aneladee Milne. Without her love of education and our communities at large, LEMI would never have had the impact it has had.

And secondly, we acknowledge you, the Mentors and LEMI Trainers, who have walked the path of being mentored and turning around and mentoring others. You inspire us. You teach us. You are affecting so many! We love you. We acknowledge the many heartfelt hours you spend mentoring. We dedicate this book to all those you love and teach.

INTRODUCTION

I thought homeschooling would be a breeze. With my background in education – years of public schooling, a master's degree, and experience teaching at the college level – I felt well-prepared. And initially, it seemed to work. My first three children adapted well to the familiar routine of workbooks, testing, and occasional fun activities.

Then came my fourth son.

Born in January, he was determined to start "real school" the moment he turned five. I eagerly pulled out my tried-and-true materials, ready to guide another child through the educational conveyor belt I knew so well. But he had other ideas. This energetic little boy loved learning but couldn't thrive while sitting still for hours. We adapted – doing math while climbing stairs, practicing reading while bouncing on a mini trampoline – but something was still missing.

Some might have labeled him my "challenging" child. I prefer to think of him as my catalyst for change. He pushed me beyond my comfortable routines and forced me to question everything I thought I knew about education. After all, wasn't my own decision to homeschool rooted in my experiences feeling invisible in traditional schools – just another number moving along the conveyor belt? Yet here I was, recreating that same system for my children.

When we moved to a new state, a friend mentioned a seminar on Leadership Education. Juggling four children (with a fifth on the way), I somehow found time to attend and devour the recommended reading. One passage stopped me in my tracks:

"Every person you have ever met is a genius. Every one. Some of us have chosen not to develop it, but it is there. It is in us. All of us. It is in your spouse. It is in each of your children. You live in a world of geniuses. How can we settle for anything less than the best education? How can we tell our children that mediocre education will do, when greatness is available?" [1]

Those words resonated deep within me. THIS was what I had been searching for! When I discovered that a mentor trained in Leadership Education was starting a homeschool community nearby through LEMI (Leadership Education Mentoring Institute), I knew I'd found my path forward. This experience with LEMI transformed not just how I approached homeschooling, but my entire perspective on education. It inspired me to pursue a second master's degree and a teaching credential, allowing me to implement these innovative learning environments across various educational settings, including private and charter schools.

My fourth son hadn't been a problem to solve. He'd been a gift, guiding our family toward a transformative approach to education.

- Heidi Christianson

For me it was a little different than it was for Heidi. I thrived in public school, except for when I didn't. And one of the ways I didn't, was the deep hunger in me that very few teachers could quench. Once in a while, I would have a teacher who gave an assignment that included a transformational experience. This usually involved a great classic, like Chaim Potak's "The Chosen,"[2] or reading the play of "Oliver Twist"[3] in elementary school. But where were the mentors who could take this little candle that had been lit and teach me how to add more fuel to keep it burning? Where were the mentors who could teach me what was happening and why a book or a song or a movie could be so moving? Who could help me sustain the change I yearned for? I would come across people in stories who felt just like me, but I didn't know what to do with the feelings I had or with the ideas I read about. I would come across behavior that had patterns but I had no language or system for deepening my understanding of "human nature" or "the natural man." All I knew is that I wanted more.

My dad knew I hungered for something. One time I told him that if I only had a photographic memory, then I could dispense with the busy work of memorizing all the stuff I spent hours on, preparing for all the tests, and get on with the important learning. He would bring me books and books from the library about memory techniques. Neither of us knew that what I needed and yearned for was around the corner. I needed a mentor – one that could give me the experiences and challenges and guidance that could lead me through the classics and one who utilized the great learning environments that accelerated change and personal growth.

And once I experienced that, starting at age 18, and on through my Master's Degree in Education, I knew there were other "kids" *like me who were searching for what I finally got – being mentored! I now burned and yearned with the desire to help make this kind of education available to families who wanted and deserved it. This was the inception of and catalyst for the creation of Leadership Education Mentoring Institute (LEMI), whose sole purpose is to make this kind of life-changing education available to all who desire it. We do this by teaching principles of leadership education that are codified as Leadership Education philosophy and methodology. A main focus and thrust has been to train mentors, both in the classroom and in the home, both liberal arts mentors and parent mentors.*

-Tiffany Earl

LEMI grew from a simple yet powerful vision: that families grow stronger, communities thrive, and lives transform when we approach education as a shared journey of growth discovery. We've seen it happen countless times – parents becoming deeply involved in their children's learning, families connecting with like-minded communities, and students discovering their unique gifts through the guidance of dedicated mentors. This isn't education in isolation; it's a vibrant tapestry woven from relationships, shared experiences, and carefully-crafted learning environments that prepare young people to make their unique mark on the world.

What do we mean by leadership? It's not about titles or positions. True leadership emerges when someone learns to navigate challenges thoughtfully, see patterns in human behavior and systems, and guide others toward positive change. It's about developing the capacity to make a meaningful difference, whether in your family, community, or broader world.

Think about the difference between learning to copy answers and learning to think deeply about questions. Traditional education often focuses on standardized instruction – moving students along a conveyor belt toward predetermined outcomes. Leadership Education takes a different path. Drawing from the Latin root "educere" – meaning "to lead out" or "draw out" – we recognize that each person carries unique potential waiting to unfold.[4] Through personalized mentoring and guided discovery, students learn not just *what* to think, but *how* to think. They develop both heart and mind, combining academic excellence with strong character. Instead of passively receiving information, they become active creators of their own learning journey, developing the confidence and capability to make meaningful contributions to their world.

The pages ahead share what we've learned about creating environments where this kind of transformative learning flourishes. Whether you're a parent hoping to nurture your children's unique gifts, a teacher seeking to inspire deeper engagement, or a mentor guiding others toward their potential, you'll find practical wisdom for moving beyond conventional education toward something truly life-changing.

For specific guidance on getting the most from this book, see the last chapter, which provides concrete strategies for implementing these environments in various educational settings along with powerful combinations and practical tips for success.

Note: Some names have been changed to protect privacy.

CHAPTER 1

The Foundation of Leadership Education: Learning Environments

Picture stepping into a classroom where students, dressed as colonial delegates, passionately debate the principles of American democracy. Or imagine watching young mathematicians light up as they grasp complex concepts through hands-on exploration. These moments reveal something crucial about learning: it's not just what we teach, but how we create the space for discovery that transforms information into understanding. These learning environments aren't simply physical spaces. They're carefully crafted experiences that shape how students connect with ideas, build skills, and grow into their potential.

Think of it like tending a garden. Just as master gardeners know that roses need different care than tomatoes, skilled educators recognize that different types of learning require distinct approaches. Some lessons bloom in the energy of group discussion, while others take root in moments of quiet reflection. Understanding how to cultivate these various learning environments becomes essential as we develop tomorrow's leaders.

Through years of experience, we've identified ten key environments that create the conditions for deep learning and personal transformation:

1. Example – Where principles come alive through actions, not just words

2. Group Discussion/Colloquia – Where ideas spark and grow through shared exploration

3. Reading – Where minds expand and perspectives shift through encounters with powerful ideas

4. Writing – Where thoughts clarify and personal voice emerges

5. Tutorial – Where personalized guidance nurtures individual growth

6. Coaching – Where focused mentorship develops both skill and character

7. Lecture – Where inspiration meets information

8. Simulations – Where theory transforms into lived experience

9. Testing, Performance, and Teaching – Where learning deepens through demonstration and sharing

10. Debrief – Where experience crystallizes into lasting wisdom

Like instruments in an orchestra, each environment plays its unique part while harmonizing with the others. When thoughtfully conducted, these environments work together to develop not just knowledgeable students, but confident, capable leaders ready to contribute meaningfully to their world.

Why Learning Environments Matter

Envision learning environments as the soil where understanding takes root and flourishes. When carefully cultivated, these environments transform education from simple information transfer into something far more powerful. They become spaces where students:

- Learn to think deeply and critically about the world around them.
- Develop not just their minds, but their hearts and character.
- Build genuine confidence through real accomplishment.
- Form meaningful connections with peers and mentors.
- See how ideas connect across subjects and into life.
- Uncover their unique gifts and passions.
- Prepare for life's real challenges through authentic experiences.

But perhaps most importantly, these environments create safe spaces where students feel free to:

- Take those crucial intellectual leaps.
- Voice half-formed ideas that might blossom into breakthrough insights.
- Make the kind of mistakes that lead to deep learning.
- Question what they thought they knew.
- Step into leadership roles, even when it feels uncomfortable.

At its heart, our careful attention to learning environments serves three vital purposes:

1. Helping students discover timeless principles they can

The Foundation of Leadership Education

apply to their own lives, not just rules to memorize, but truths they've tested and proven for themselves.

2.   Developing a student's ability to think critically about different approaches to life's challenges – what we call "comparing forms." This means learning to recognize patterns in how different choices lead to different outcomes.

3.   Empowering students to discover and pursue their unique missions in life; not just careers, but their authentic ways of contributing to the world.

These environments don't just shape what students learn, they shape who students become.

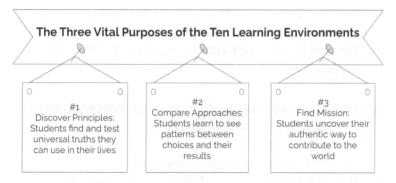

The Three Vital Purposes of the Ten Learning Environments

#1
Discover Principles:
Students find and test universal truths they can use in their lives

#2
Compare Approaches:
Students learn to see patterns between choices and their results

#3
Find Mission:
Students uncover their authentic way to contribute to the world

Beyond Physical Space

Consider learning environments as something far richer than just the physical spaces where we teach. They're more like invisible gardens where minds and hearts grow, shaped by the quality of our relationships, the depth of our conversations, and the spirit of discovery we cultivate together. Mentors, like skilled gardeners, nurture these environments by:

- Setting clear expectations that encourage growth.
- Modeling the curiosity and character they hope to inspire.
- Creating safe spaces where new ideas can take root.
- Adapting their approach to each student's unique needs.
- Maintaining an atmosphere where learning thrives.
- Guiding students skillfully through different ways of learning.

BEYOND PHYSICAL SPACE

In these pages, besides learning to effectively administer and facilitate a variety of key learning environments, mentors will also discover how to:

- Be still, and in the quiet moments imagine themselves as their individual students, deeply understanding where they are now as well as who they can become.

The Foundation of Leadership Education

- Utilize the Leadership Ladders to help identify the students' roadblocks and find solutions.
- Understand each person's role on the leadership education team.
- Fine-tune the assignments to fit each student's needs.
- Inspire the students to take responsibility for their job of being educable.

That's the beauty of Leadership Education – it flourishes in all sorts of settings when effective mentoring takes place. We've seen this adaptable approach work wonderfully in:

- Individual homes, where parents tailor education to each child's spark.
- Homeschool communities, where families come together for shared learning adventures.
- Liber Communities, where deep relationships and education flourish from collaborative efforts to offer a leadership education.
- Micro schools, where small class sizes enable truly personalized attention.

In homeschool communities, families discover the power of working together – sharing teaching gifts, organizing joint classes, planning field trips, and creating workshops that benefit everyone's children.

Liber Communities take this collaboration even further. They create spaces where independent thinking flourishes through rich discussions, Socratic seminars, and group projects. Here, mentors and students challenge each other to reach higher while staying grounded in strong values and moral character.

Micro schools offer another wonderful option, combining the intimacy of small classes with the flexibility to partner with other families for specialized learning opportunities.

But the real magic happens in how these different environments connect and strengthen each other. When educators share what works, tackle challenges together, and combine their gifts in joint projects, students encounter a richer variety of perspectives and opportunities. Whether learning happens at home, in community centers, or in traditional classrooms, mentors weave these environments together to build confidence, spark creativity, and help students take charge of their own learning journey.

The goal stays constant: creating spaces where real learning takes root and personal growth blooms naturally.

Setting the Stage for Success

Imagine what lies ahead as an exciting journey of discovery. We'll begin by understanding the natural Phases of Learning, from Discovery Phase through Scholar Phase, recognizing how students progress in their educational journey. This foundation helps us meet students where they are developmentally.

Next, we'll explore two essential tools of effective mentoring. First, we'll learn to develop our "spiritual eyes" - the ability to truly see and understand our students. Then we'll discover how to use the Leadership Ladders to spot where growth is needed and guide that growth effectively.

Think of these as the navigator's twin tools: Spiritual Eyes help us see where students really are, while Leadership Ladders provide the map showing possible paths forward.

With this foundation established, we'll meet the key players who bring Leadership Education to life - students, mentors, parents, peers, and even the educational content itself. Just like a beautifully performed play needs every actor to understand their role, Leadership Education happens when everyone involved knows how they contribute.

Finally, we'll dive deep into each learning environment, providing you with both the "why" and the "how" - practical tools you can use whether you're teaching at your kitchen table, leading in a classroom, or mentoring tomorrow's leaders in your community. Creating powerful learning experiences is a foundation of mentoring. We will cover what makes each environment effective and how to use them.

As you explore these environments and get to know the people who bring them to life, you'll develop an instinct for choosing just the right approach for each learning moment.

Let's Take a Deeper Look — Chapter I

These questions aren't just for pondering – they're invitations to connect these ideas with your own journey and vision as an educator. Take time to explore them deeply, perhaps journaling your thoughts or discussing them with fellow mentors.

1. Think back to a moment that changed how you learn or think. Maybe it was an inspiring teacher, a challenging project, or an unexpected discovery. What made that experience so powerful?

2. Imagine two different paths: one where students move along a conveyor belt receiving information, and another where their unique gifts are drawn out and developed. How does this shift change everything – from how students see themselves to how we create learning experiences? What becomes possible when we focus on "leading out" rather than just "pouring in"?

3. As you look at these ten learning environments, which ones feel like old friends, and which seem like exciting new territory? Think about your comfort zone as a mentor or learner. How might stretching into those less familiar environments open up new possibilities for growth – both for you and your students?

4. We've explored how learning environments go far beyond physical spaces. When we think of them as

The Foundation of Leadership Education

carefully crafted experiences, how does that shift your view of what's possible in facilitating a Leadership Education? What new doors open when we're not limited by traditional ideas of "classroom" or "lesson"?

5. Let's consider leadership – not as a position, but as a capacity for meaningful impact. How do you see yourself as a leader as you mentor others?

6. Why do the three vital purposes for the Learning Environments matter to you?

Resources for Deeper Learning:

LEMIWorks! Podcast – found on most podcast platforms and at LEMIWorks.com[1]

LEMI Essential Foundations Online Course - free and available on LEMI-U.com[2]

CHAPTER 2

The Phases of Learning

Visualize a child learning to walk. First they crawl, then wobble upright, take tentative steps, and finally run with confidence. Learning follows similar natural progressions – distinct phases that build upon each other as students grow and develop. Understanding these phases helps us nurture growth at just the right pace, like knowing when to hold a child's hand and when to let them explore independently.

What we often forget as parent mentors, classroom mentors, and teachers, is that a lot of mistakes go into learning to crawl, then pulling oneself upright, then taking steps. Hundreds of failures happen. No child crawls or walks without them. And this process continues through the Phases of Learning. We learn by exploring, doing, failing, and doing again. We get some parts right and others wrong. And eventually we are running.

The journey unfolds through several key phases:

1. Discovery Phase (Ages 0-11)

2. Scholar Phase (Ages 12-18)[1], which includes:
   - Practice Scholar (~12-14 years)
   - Apprentice Scholar (~14-16 years)
   - Self-Directed Scholar (~14-18 years)

3. Depth Phase[2]

4. Mission Phase[3]

Remember, these ages are guidelines, not rigid boundaries. Just as some children walk at nine months while others take their first steps at fifteen months, each student progresses through these phases at their own perfect pace. So please don't let yourself get caught up in the age transitions, trust the actual process of growth. Let's dive deeper into each phase.

THE PHASES OF LEARNING

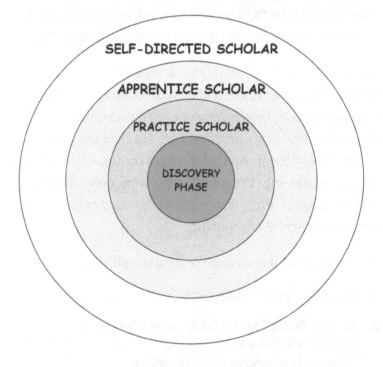

The Discovery Phase forms the core of Leadership Education, much like a tree's innermost rings. Its emphasis on character and curiosity remains active as students advance through Scholar phases, with each phase building upon and strengthening previous learning.

While they fall outside this book's focus on earlier educational phases, it's worth briefly noting that students typically progress to two additional phases. The Depth Phase occurs during college years, characterized by intensive study and sophisticated mastery within specific disciplines.[4] This is followed by the Mission Phase, where individuals apply their knowledge and expertise to make meaningful contributions in their fields and communities through teaching, creating, leading, or problem-solving.[5]

The Discovery Phase: Two Key Focuses (Ages 0-11)

Picture a toddler encountering a butterfly for the first time. Her eyes widen with wonder as she reaches out, trying to touch its delicate wings. This simple moment captures the essence of the Discovery Phase – a time when children naturally blend an insatiable curiosity about their world while developing character. If the child succeeds in grasping the butterfly, the child learns that the butterfly was harmed and learns a lesson about life.

The Discovery Phase (ages 0-11) weaves together two beautiful threads of early childhood: the development of character and the blossoming of natural curiosity. Think of them as dance partners, moving in harmony to create something greater than either could achieve alone.

The first thread – natural curiosity – unfolds like a flower opening to the sun. I remember watching my son discover shadows for the first time. What started as simple handwaving evolved into complex experiments with light and objects, each discovery fueling his desire to learn more. This natural drive to understand their world leads children from simple "what's that?" questions to deeper explorations of how things work and why they happen.

The second thread – character development – grows through everyday moments. It's there in the gentle "thank you" a child learns to say, in the comfort of family routines, and in the freedom to play and explore safely. Rather than pushing academic achievements, we focus on nurturing their emotional security and moral compass. We've watched children in this phase develop deep wells of empathy and understanding simply through living life alongside caring adults who model these qualities.

These threads intertwine from the very beginning. An infant discovering her hands isn't just learning about fingers and movement, she's also building confidence and joy in discovery. A preschooler sharing toys isn't only developing social skills, he's also exploring cause and effect through others' reactions.

What makes this phase so powerful is how it honors each child's unique journey. Some might dive deeply into building things while others spend hours observing insects. The key isn't directing their path but creating rich environments where both character and curiosity can flourish naturally. Our job as mentors is to facilitate these environments by both listening to our children's natural curiosities and desires as well as trusting our own gifts and interests.

The Discovery Phase celebrates:

- The quiet moments when a child chooses kindness without prompting.
- The excited "aha!" when something finally makes sense.
- The peaceful confidence that comes from feeling emotionally secure.
- The sparkle in their eyes when discovering something new.
- The natural development of critical thinking through play and exploration.
- The joy that emerges when learning feels like an adventure.
- The wonder that makes ordinary moments extraordinary.

Remember, we're not building a foundation with rigid blocks, we're tending a garden where character and curiosity grow together, each supporting and enriching the other in beautiful and unexpected ways.

Scholar Phase: Advanced Learning

Imagine watching a butterfly emerge from its chrysalis. The transformation doesn't happen all at once. It's a gradual unfolding, each stage essential to the creature's development. The Scholar Phase follows a similar pattern of beautiful metamorphosis.[6]

I'll never forget watching Sarah, one of my students, transition into this phase. One day, while discussing the

American Revolution, she suddenly sat up straighter, her eyes bright with a new kind of engagement. She wasn't just absorbing information anymore. She was beginning to wrestle with ideas, to question assumptions, to think critically about the world around her. This is the magic of the Scholar Phase.

This remarkable period typically begins around adolescence, building upon the wonder and character developed in earlier years. Like a skilled architect adding new floors to a solid foundation, scholars begin constructing their own understanding through independent research, thoughtful analysis, and rich discussions with peers. They're not just learning facts, they're developing the tools to become lifelong learners and future leaders.

The journey unfolds through three distinct stages, each with its own flavor:

- Practice Scholars (around 12-14) are like assistant chefs learning to use basic tools.
- Apprentice Scholars (roughly 14-16) begin cooking independently.
- Self-Directed Scholars (approximately 14-18) begin crafting their own recipes.

But here's the beautiful thing: there's no rigid timeline. Each scholar develops at their own pace. I've seen twelve-year-olds dive into Practice Scholar work with remarkable maturity, while others might need an extra year to find their footing. One of my most impressive scholars spent three years in the Practice phase, building a rock-solid foundation that later launched her into incredible academic achievements.

Consider these age ranges as gentle guidelines rather than strict rules. What matters isn't when a student enters each phase, but that they're given the time and support to develop fully within it. After all, we're not running a race – we're nurturing future leaders who can think deeply, reason clearly, and contribute meaningfully to their world.

Interconnectedness of Phases

Picture a garden through the seasons, each flowing naturally into the next while carrying forward earlier growth. The phases of learning work much the same way, weaving together in a continuous journey of development.

I learned this through Marcus, whose Discovery Phase fascination with butterflies naturally evolved into Scholar Phase research on migration patterns. The observation skills he developed chasing butterflies became the foundation for his scientific investigations – a perfect example of how each phase enriches the others.

This interconnection becomes crucial when choosing how to teach. A formal Socratic discussion that engages Self-Directed Scholars might overwhelm Practice Scholars, while hands-on activities perfect for Discovery Phase students might need to be followed by a document study and comparative essay in order to challenge Apprentice Scholars enough. Understanding these natural progressions helps us use our "spiritual eyes" to match learning environments to developmental stages.

Think of it like building a house – Scholar Phase adds new rooms on top of the existing structure. The emotional security and wonder developed in Discovery Phase enrich Scholar Phase studies. The curiosity cultivated through early exploration fuels later research and understanding.

Understanding Discovery Phase students versus Scholar Phase students guides us in implementing learning environments effectively:

- Simulations might need different complexity levels for different phases.
- Group discussions may require varying degrees of length.
- Lectures might need adjustment in length and interaction level.

By recognizing these natural connections, we can provide just the right environment at just the right time, supported by the Leadership Ladders (VMASK) – Vision, Mission, Abilities, Skills, and Knowledge – which help us identify exactly what each student needs next for growth.

Let's Take a Deeper Look – Chapter 2

These questions aren't just for pondering – they're invitations to connect these ideas with your own journey and vision as an educator. Take time to explore them deeply, perhaps journaling your thoughts or discussing them with fellow mentors.

1. The chapter describes the Discovery Phase as weaving together two threads: natural curiosity and character development. Think about a child you know in this phase. How have you seen these threads interacting in their development?

2. Consider the progression through the Scholar Phase (Practice Scholar, Apprentice Scholar, Self-Directed Scholar). How might this gradual increase in independence and responsibility help prepare students for real-world leadership?

3. The chapter emphasizes that ages for different phases are guidelines, not rigid boundaries. Reflect on your own educational journey or that of someone you know. How did your/their progression through these phases align with or differ from the suggested ages? What factors influenced this timing?

4. Looking at the interconnectedness of phases, how might early experiences in the Discovery Phase (ages 0-11) lay the groundwork for later success in the Scholar Phase?

What specific qualities or habits developed in Discovery Phase could support scholarly work?

5. The chapter mentions that "a lot of mistakes go into learning." How might understanding this principle change how we approach education?

Resources for Deeper Learning:

> **Leadership Education: The Phases of Learning,** by Oliver and Rachel DeMille[7]

> **LEMI Mentor Training** - a three day immersive program where participants are trained in project-based learning, Leadership Education and the Learning Environments. For more information go to LEMIHomeschool.com

CHAPTER 3

Guiding Growth through Spiritual Eyes and the Leadership Ladders

Envision the most attentive gardener you know – someone who notices the slightest change in their plants, who can tell by a single leaf what is needed to thrive. As mentors, teachers, and parents, we're called to develop this same deep attentiveness to the young minds and hearts in our care. Our role isn't just to teach, but to truly see the unique potential waiting to unfold in each student.

This kind of seeing goes beyond surface observation. We call it developing "spiritual eyes" – the ability to perceive not just who our students are today, but who they have the capacity to become. Imagine being able to step so completely into a student's shoes that you can feel what they feel, see what they see, and understand exactly what they need to take their next step forward. This isn't about making assumptions; it's about developing such deep understanding that you can recognize precisely what each student needs in order to grow.

Think about watching a master chef teach an apprentice. They don't just demonstrate techniques; they seem to know intuitively when to encourage, when to challenge, when to step back and let the learner discover something for themselves. That's what we're aiming for: the ability to recognize what the student needs when they come to a roadblock. There is a balance between knowing how to guide them to their next step and knowing when to get out of their way while they get to work.

This kind of mentoring requires us to slow down, to be still, to really see each student's particular circumstances, needs, and learning style. Sometimes that means letting go of our carefully planned lessons to follow where a student's curiosity leads. Other times it means gently guiding them back to a challenge they're trying to avoid. Always, it means resisting the temptation to apply one-size-fits-all solutions to deeply individual journeys.

After all, learning isn't a production line where we can stamp out identical results. It's more like tending a diverse garden, where each plant needs its own specific combination of sun, shade, water, and nutrients to flourish. Our job is to create the conditions where each unique individual can grow into their fullest potential.

Developing Spiritual Eyes

Think back to a time when someone truly saw your potential – not just who you were in that moment, but who you could become. As mentors, that's our most sacred task: recognizing and nurturing the unique gifts within each student. We call this ability "spiritual eyes" – seeing beyond the surface to understand not only the current challenges, but exactly what each student needs to move past them.

Two remarkable stories show us different facets of

developing these spiritual eyes. Each offers powerful insights into how we can deepen our ability to truly see and guide our students.

The Story of Suzuki and the Blind Student

When parents asked Shinichi Suzuki to teach their blind son violin, he didn't rush to say yes. Instead, he took a week to prepare in an extraordinary way. He went to his office, closed the shutters, and immersed himself in darkness. There, in the blackness, he played his violin, discovering how to teach without relying on sight.[1]

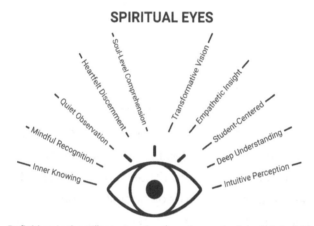

SPIRITUAL EYES

Soul-Level Comprehension
Heartfelt Discernment
Transformative Vision
Quiet Observation
Empathetic Insight
Mindful Recognition
Student-Centered
Inner Knowing
Deep Understanding
Intuitive Perception

Definition: In the stillness, sensing the unique potential within individuals and perceiving the next step needed for progression and growth.

When lessons finally began, Suzuki didn't start with the violin. Instead, he taught the boy to "see" with his mind's eye. He guided the child's hands over the bow, then asked simply, "Can you see it?" The boy's confident "Yes!" marked a breakthrough moment – he had learned to see through touch and imagination, while Suzuki had learned to teach through truly understanding his student's world.

Enzio Busche's Life-Changing Awakening

Our second story takes us to a very different time and place. Enzio Busche, a former Hitler Youth, found himself hospitalized in his early twenties facing a life-threatening condition. In what he called a moment of "complete recognition," he saw his life with startling clarity. Looking at his simple hospital blanket, he was suddenly overwhelmed by all he had taken for granted – the sheep that provided the wool, the hands that spun and dyed it, the countless hours of work that went into creating something he had never truly appreciated.[2]

This profound awakening transformed how Busche saw everything – from life's simplest blessings to his deepest relationships. He promised himself that if he survived, he would live with "complete awareness of conscience," approaching life with new gratitude and insight. His story challenges us as mentors to look honestly at ourselves and our impact on others. After all, how can we guide students toward this kind of self-awareness if we're not willing to develop it ourselves?

Together, these stories reveal two essential truths about developing spiritual eyes: we must learn to see from our students' perspectives while also having the courage to see ourselves clearly. It's this combination – deep empathy and honest self-reflection – that enables us to truly understand

and guide our students toward their potential.

Understanding how to use these spiritual eyes effectively requires what we call the Leadership Ladders. Like a compass, this tool helps us spot both where students are and what they need next. The Leadership Ladders guide us in creating learning environments and educational challenges that meet each student exactly where they are while leading them toward where they could be.

The Leadership Ladders

Imagine trying to help someone climb a mountain without knowing which path they're on or what equipment they need. That's what mentoring can feel like without the right tools. This is where the Leadership Ladders come in. They are five building blocks that help us guide each student's unique journey of growth.

I remember the day this clicked for me. Kimberly sat in my classroom, clearly struggling with her writing assignment. My first instinct was to dive into grammar rules and essay structure. But something made me pause and really look – not just at her paper, but at her. Using the Leadership Ladders as my guide, I realized she didn't need more writing techniques. She needed to find her voice, to believe her stories were worth telling. She needed Vision before Skills.

Developed through decades of observation and practice at the Leadership Education Mentoring Institute, these ladders offer a different approach than the typical "one-size-fits-all" education. They remind us to be still, to truly see our students. Think of a holistic doctor who doesn't just treat symptoms but takes time to understand the whole person. That's what these ladders help us do – see beyond the surface to what each student truly needs in the moment.

When we understand these five pathways of growth – Vision, Mission, Abilities, Skills, and Knowledge – we can name the real roadblock and then ascertain the right step for moving forward. Instead of just delivering information, we create experiences that touch hearts, awaken minds, and nurture authentic growth.

Imagine a young climber facing a rock wall. Several things are happening at once. And if one of them isn't working, the climber cannot ascend. The climber has to know where they are headed and why (VISION). They have to want to go up (MISSION). They need to be harnessed correctly and have a skilled belayer (SKILLS) they trust and the strength to pull and climb (ABILITIES). They need the knowledge to know where to place their hands and feet (KNOWLEDGE).

We call these crucial systems the Leadership Ladders – five distinct ladders that are happening simultaneously in order for growth to occur. Learning is essentially navigating through and overcoming roadblocks. Naming the roadblock is half the work. The other half is doing the work, once it's named. If one of these crucial ladders is blocked, the mentor and the student work together to discover which it is and then do the work to fix it. This is how mentors guide their students. They have climbed this wall. They have the vision and they share it. They know it's worth it and have a strong why. And they do their best to transfer the fire and awaken the desire for the climb. The mentor also knows the harness and the ropes and so can identify if there is a problem and can direct the student in how to solve it. As far as having the strength to cimb, the student must develop those muscles themselves through practice and use. And of course it is effort that delivers the knowledge of where to place hands and feet on the ascent.

We've seen mentors transform countless students over the years by understanding these Ladders. We know them by the acronym V-MASK, and each one serves a unique purpose in a student's development:

Vision – Picture Thomas, a bright student who could solve complex math problems but saw no point in doing so. "Why does this matter?" he'd ask. That's when I knew we needed to start with Vision. Just as a lighthouse guides ships home, Vision answers our deepest "why" questions: Why study Shakespeare? Why master mathematics? Why develop good habits? Without this guiding light, even the most talented students can lose their way.

Mission – Then there's Emma, who excelled in everything but couldn't see her own unique worth. Helping her discover her potential to contribute something special to the world transformed not just her studies, but her entire approach to learning. Each individual has something unique to offer and has inherent worth.

Abilities – Consider James, technically brilliant but struggling to work with others. His journey wasn't about learning more facts. It was about developing character qualities like empathy, integrity, and patience.

Skills – Or Maria, whose passion for writing was limited by her technical abilities. She needed concrete tools and techniques such as character development, world building, and story type to bring her stories to life.

Knowledge – Finally, there's David, whose curiosity about history was hampered by gaps in his basic understanding. He needed the vocabulary and context to dive deeper into his interests.

We must learn to recognize which ladder our students need most when they get stuck. Sometimes we need to look deeply and listen closely. Sometimes a student stuck on skill acquisition actually needs Vision first. Other times, what looks like a Knowledge gap might really be a Mission question.

By learning to see these distinctions – using our spiritual eyes, as we call it – we can offer exactly the support each student needs, when they need it. It's like having a map that shows not just where students are, but the best path forward for their unique journey. After helping the student name and solve the roadblock, it is important to get out of the student's way while they work. It is also important to remember that part of their work includes making mistakes and learning from them. Mistakes and successes are part of their growth. It is not our job to do their thinking for them or to stop them from practicing even when they get it wrong sometimes. This is how students learn to trust themselves and how to trust that it's okay not to be perfect. Growth requires a lot of kinds of work, including making mistakes.

Let's dive deeper into how each of these ladders works in practice, and how we can help our students climb them successfully.

Ladder #1: Vision

I once watched a student named Michael stare at his algebra homework with complete disinterest. "When will I ever use this?" he sighed. It wasn't that he couldn't do the math. He simply couldn't see why he should bother. Without vision, even the brightest students can lose their way.

Think of vision as the North Star of learning. Just as ancient sailors needed that guiding light to navigate vast oceans, our students need a compelling "why" to guide them through their educational journey. Why study Shakespeare? Why master mathematics? Why develop daily habits of excellence? Vision answers these essential questions, transforming "have to" into "want to."

Remember Suzuki's transformative moment with the blind student learning violin? The boy's parents obviously had a vision for their son. They had probably seen a spark in him when they played music at home. They even knew that Suzuki was a master violin teacher. They hoped beyond hope that perhaps he could teach their son, despite his blindness. Suzuki had to get his own vision of what was possible. That is why he took a week before he answered. He needed to know what was possible. By imagining being blind himself, and being able to play beautifully, he knew a blind child could play the violin. He also knew what skills the boy would need. He would need to be able to imagine seeing the bow and violin in his mind's eye. Then he would need to successfully learn to move the bow across horizontally and then vertically. Each step was practiced over and over until the boy could control the bow. By starting with vision – helping the boy "see" the violin in his mind before touching it – Suzuki demonstrated a profound truth about learning. [3]

When students can envision something clearly, even if they can't physically see it, they connect with it at a deeper level. Just as that young student moved from "seeing" to truly understanding the violin, our students need to envision the purpose and possibility in their learning before they can fully engage with it.

As mentors, our first responsibility is to light this spark of vision. When I see a student struggling, I've learned to ask myself: "Have I helped them see the stars they're steering by? Have I shown them why this journey matters?"

The art of vision-casting is like painting a picture of possibility. It means:

- Revealing the "why" behind the lesson.
- Weaving connections to students' lives and dreams.
- Building bridges between today's effort and tomorrow's possibilities.
- Showing how learning opens doors in the real world.

I use the "Know, Feel, Do" compass to guide my vision-casting:

- Know: What understanding do I hope will light up their minds?
- Feel: What emotions might kindle their passion for learning?
- Do: What actions could this knowledge inspire?

You know vision has taken root when you see the signs: eyes lighting up with curiosity, conversations spilling beyond class time, connections being made across subjects. My favorite moment is when students start sharing their enthusiasm with others. That's when I know they've caught the vision for themselves.

One of my students captured it perfectly: "It's like suddenly seeing in color when everything was gray before." That's the power of vision – it transforms learning from a task to complete into a journey to embrace.

Ladder #2: Mission

I'll never forget Rebecca's transformation. She sat in my classroom, brilliant but believing she had nothing unique to offer the world. Then one day, we studied Marie Curie. As Rebecca learned about this remarkable woman who revolutionized science despite countless obstacles, something shifted. "If she could change the world through her passion for science," Rebecca whispered, "maybe my love of chemistry matters too."

This is the heart of Mission – understanding that each student carries a unique gift for the world. Like fingerprints, no two students' purposes are exactly alike. Some might be called to heal, others to create, still others to build or teach or inspire. And just as seasons change, these missions often evolve throughout life, offering many ways to contribute meaningfully to the world.

Sometimes students discover their mission through moments of inspiration – hearing a piece of music that moves their soul, encountering art that takes their breath away, or learning about people who dared to make a difference. It's like watching a candle flame jump from one wick to another. Suddenly, possibility ignites.

But what about students who can't see their own light? Their doubt often masks itself in troubling ways: distraction, anxiety, withdrawal from others. While we can't force students to recognize their worth, we can reflect it back to them consistently, like mirrors helping them see their own brightness.

Remember the story of Enzio Busche shared earlier – how a hospital stay became his awakening to purpose. His realization that even a simple blanket represented countless hands working together transformed his understanding of human worth and potential.[4] Our students need similar awakenings to their own significance.

We've learned to watch for signs that a student is struggling with Mission. When Emily started skipping class, it wasn't about the subject matter; she couldn't see how her unique perspective mattered. By sharing stories of others who found their purpose, helping her explore her natural gifts, and consistently believing in her potential, we helped Emily rediscover her spark.

Because here's the truth: when someone doesn't fulfill their mission, it's not just their loss. The whole world misses out on a gift that only they could give.

Ladder #3: Abilities; and Ladder #4: Skills

I once watched two students tackle the same challenging math problem. Both were equally talented, but their approaches revealed a striking difference. Marcus had all the technical skills but gave up at the first setback. Emma, though still developing her mathematical abilities, persisted with determination and creativity, eventually finding the solution. This moment crystallized for me the crucial difference between Skills and Abilities.

Think of Skills as the tools in our toolbox – the technical "how-to" of any subject or task. Abilities? They're more like the steady hand that guides those tools, shaped by character qualities like kindness, honesty, and fortitude. As Joshua Cooper Ramo wisely noted, "Our greatest weapon will not be our bombers, our drones, or our financial strength. It will be our own humanity"[5] and "So we find our future not in our own hands, but instead in the grip of two groups, one ignorant of networks, the other ignorant of humanity. The only answer, then, is to educate ourselves."[6] In the challenges we face, our human qualities—such as empathy, resilience, and integrity—will be our greatest assets.

Remember our mentor Suzuki and his remarkable work with violin students. In his graduation tape feedback, you can hear this delicate dance between Skills and Abilities. Consider these two moments:

"Lower your right elbow slightly" – a precise technical correction to improve violin technique. Pure Skill.

But then listen to how he addresses something deeper: "Today your music tells me you're feeling disobedient." Here, Suzuki reaches beyond technique to touch the heart of character development. The realm of Abilities.

I saw this principle at work recently with Sarah, a gifted writer whose beautiful prose masked a reluctance to accept criticism. Her technical skills were impressive, but her ability to handle feedback – to grow from it rather than withdraw – needed nurturing. Just as Suzuki guided his students to practice saying "yes" instead of "no," we worked on developing Sarah's resilience alongside her writing craft.

As mentors, our challenge is to see clearly which ladder needs our attention. Is it a true skill gap – like not understanding paragraph structure? Or is it an ability challenge – like lacking the confidence to express original ideas? Sometimes what looks like a skill problem has ability roots, and vice versa.

The goal isn't just to create technically proficient students, but to nurture well-rounded individuals who combine competence with character. After all, in life's greatest challenges, it's often our human qualities – our Abilities – that matter most.

Ladder #5: Knowledge

Sometimes the simplest explanation is the right one. I remember puzzling over why Michael, usually eager to participate in science discussions, had grown quiet. After several attempts to engage him, I realized he was missing some basic vocabulary – terms like "velocity" and "acceleration" were fuzzy in his mind. Once we filled these knowledge gaps, his natural curiosity returned, and he dove back into our experiments with renewed enthusiasm.

Knowledge might be the last rung on our ladder, but it's far from the least important. Think of it as the rich soil from which understanding grows. I love watching this process unfold, like the journey of Anna, one of my former students who fell in love with horticulture. At first, plant anatomy was just a list of terms to memorize. But as her knowledge deepened, something beautiful happened. Suddenly she could explain why that patch of grass was yellowing, or exactly when to prune the peach trees for the best harvest.

Her knowledge had transformed from abstract facts into living wisdom she could share with others.

Language often holds the key to this transformation. We encourage our students to become collectors of words and concepts – not just memorizing definitions, but truly understanding the ideas they represent. It's like building a toolkit: each new term or concept becomes another tool for understanding the world more deeply.

When I notice a student struggling, one of my questions is, "Do they have the basic knowledge needed here?" Sometimes what is needed is simply understanding. Just as you can't build a house without a foundation, you can't engage deeply with ideas without basic knowledge of the subject to support them.

The beauty of the Knowledge ladder is that it's always there, ready to be climbed. Whether it's mastering the vocabulary of physics or understanding the intricate dance of plant growth cycles, building knowledge creates confidence and capability that ripples through every other aspect of learning.

Applying the Leadership Ladders

Let me share a classroom moment that brought the Leadership Ladders to life. It was discussion day for a book I'd assigned, and as hands went up indicating who hadn't finished reading, I saw an opportunity to put these five ladders into practice.

Picture John, slumped in his chair, offering a dismissive, "It was boring" when asked why he hadn't read the book. His response was like a mirror, reflecting back my own oversight – I hadn't cast a clear vision for why this book mattered. But as I listened more deeply, I realized John's challenge wasn't just about vision. He also needed practical skills for tackling challenging texts, like knowing when to skim and how to handle unfamiliar words. His situation reminded me that our students climb multiple ladders simultaneously.

Then there was Bart, who claimed he "didn't have time." Any mentor recognizes this familiar refrain, but his words pointed to something deeper – an Abilities challenge around time management and personal discipline. It wasn't just about scheduling; it was about developing the character to honor commitments and distinguish between urgent and important tasks. I made a mental note that a lesson in time management might benefit the entire class.

Melissa's dismissal of the book as "stupid" caught my attention. Her words hinted at a Mission ladder challenge. She couldn't see how this learning connected to her unique purpose in the world. She needed to see herself in the story, to understand how this book might illuminate her own path forward.

As I worked with each student, patterns emerged. John needed both Vision to spark interest and Skills to navigate complex texts. Bart required Abilities development in time management. Melissa needed to connect with her sense of

Mission. And underlying everything was Knowledge – whether that meant building vocabulary, understanding time management strategies, or discovering connections between the book and personal interests.

This experience reminded me why I love these ladders. They're not just theoretical tools. They're practical guides that help us see beneath surface struggles to core needs. When we identify the right ladder, we can offer exactly the support each student needs to climb higher.

The joy comes in watching students discover their path forward. John eventually found his way into the book through a character who shared his passion for adventure. Bart developed a simple but effective planning system. And Melissa? She ended up leading our most animated discussion when she discovered how the book's themes paralleled her own questions about purpose.

Even in the Scholar Projects (time tested Leadership Education projects that help move students through Scholar Phase) that utilize the Learning Environments taught in this book, mentors have to use their Spiritual Eyes to determine the "secondary lessons" based on the V-MASK needs of the class. No one else can completely do that for you as the mentor of your class. Understanding the Leadership Ladders helps you craft these lessons that are unique to your students.

Leadership Ladders Examples

Picture a mentor trying to help a struggling student. Without these ladders, it's like trying to diagnose an engine problem without knowing how engines work. But with them? Everything changes. When a student hits a roadblock, the roadblock will be in one of these five categories: Vision, Mission, Abilities, Skills, or Knowledge.

It's so exciting to see the ladders in action. A student who seemed completely stuck suddenly blossomed when we realized she didn't need more skill practice. What she needed was to catch the vision of why her work mattered. That's the magic of the Leadership Ladders developed by LEMI. They help us see exactly where a student needs support:

- Vision: Are their eyes lit up with purpose?
- Mission: Can they see how this connects to their unique path?
- Abilities: Do they need to develop certain character traits?
- Skills: Are specific competencies missing?
- Knowledge: Do they need foundational understanding?

LEMI has crafted specific objectives for the ladders for each project and phase, while encouraging mentors to create additional ones for their unique classroom needs. Think of them as a mentor's secret decoder ring, helping us understand exactly what each student needs to thrive.

Ready to explore how these ladders work their magic through different phases? Let's dive into the journey from Discovery Phase through Scholar Phase, where each step builds on the last in a beautiful progression of growth.

Discovery Phase Ladders (Ages 0-11)

When my youngest was four, he spent hours watching ants march across our backyard, completely absorbed in their tiny world. At first, I worried he was "falling behind" in traditional academic skills. But through LEMI's Discovery Phase Leadership Ladders, I began to see these moments differently – not as distractions from learning, but as precious building blocks of curiosity and wonder and the development of deep focus.

The Discovery Phase Leadership Ladders provide a framework for nurturing young learners during their foundational years. These ladders reflect our understanding that early education should focus on awakening wonder, building character, and developing essential life skills, rather than just academic achievement. Each ladder addresses a crucial aspect of development, from inspiring curiosity and recognizing personal worth to mastering basic skills and understanding fundamental truths about the world.

These ladders are intentionally broad and flexible, allowing mentors to adapt them to each child's unique needs and pace of development. Rather than presenting a rigid checklist, they offer guideposts for mentors to ensure balanced growth across all areas. The emphasis at this level is on creating positive associations with learning, building strong character foundations, and developing basic tools for future scholarship.

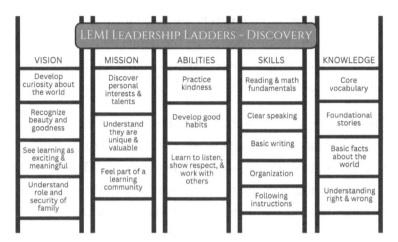

VISION	MISSION	ABILITIES	SKILLS	KNOWLEDGE
Develop curiosity about the world	Discover personal interests & talents	Practice kindness	Reading & math fundamentals	Core vocabulary
Recognize beauty and goodness	Understand they are unique & valuable	Develop good habits	Clear speaking	Foundational stories
See learning as exciting & meaningful		Learn to listen, show respect, & work with others	Basic writing	Basic facts about the world
Understand role and security of family	Feel part of a learning community		Organization	Understanding right & wrong
			Following instructions	

LEMI LEADERSHIP LADDERS - DISCOVERY

As you use these ladders, remember that progress often comes in small steps and may not always be linear. The goal is steady growth in each area while maintaining the joy and wonder that characterize effective Discovery Phase Learning.

These Discovery Phase Leadership Ladders lay the groundwork for the more structured ladders students will encounter in their Scholar Phase while honoring the unique needs and natural development patterns of younger learners.

Practice Scholar Ladders

The Practice Scholar Leadership Ladders guide students through their initial transition into scholarly work, typically around ages 12-14. This phase focuses primarily on testing initiative, giving students the freedom to discover their own drive for learning and growth. With approximately 15-25 hours of weekly discretionary time to study what interests them along side approximately 25-30 hours of academic work, students begin developing the habits and understanding that will serve them throughout their scholarly journey.

These ladders reflect a crucial developmental stage where students start moving beyond simple curiosity to deeper engagement with ideas and their own potential. The emphasis shifts from external motivation to internal drive, helping students discover not just what they're capable of doing but who they're capable of becoming. Each ladder addresses specific aspects of this development, from understanding their relationship with country, self, and God, to mastering basic scholarly skills and exploring fundamental life questions.

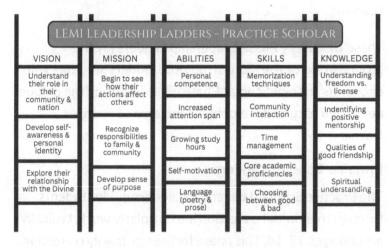

VISION	MISSION	ABILITIES	SKILLS	KNOWLEDGE
Understand their role in their community & nation	Begin to see how their actions affect others	Personal competence	Memorization techniques	Understanding freedom vs. license
		Increased attention span	Community interaction	Indentifying positive mentorship
Develop self-awareness & personal identity	Recognize responsibilities to family & community	Growing study hours	Time management	Qualities of good friendship
Explore their relationship with the Divine	Develop sense of purpose	Self-motivation	Core academic proficiencies	Spiritual understanding
		Language (poetry & prose)	Choosing between good & bad	

The Practice Scholar phase is aptly named – it's a time for students to practice taking initiative in their learning while still having the safety net of mentor guidance. These ladders help mentors strike the delicate balance between providing structure and allowing students the freedom to develop their own motivation and work ethic.

As students progress through these ladders, they build the foundation necessary for more rigorous scholarly work in the Apprentice Scholar phase. The focus is not on perfection but on developing the initiative, understanding, and basic skills that will support future academic and personal growth.

Apprentice Scholar Ladders

Picture Sarah, fifteen, standing before her peers to present her research on the Constitutional Convention. Her hands might have trembled slightly, but her voice rang clear as she connected the Founders' struggles with modern challenges. This moment – this transformation from student to scholar – captures the essence of LEMI's Apprentice Scholar phase.

At ages 14-16, something remarkable happens. Like apprentice craftsmen of old, these students begin dedicating themselves to their work with new intensity – about 40 hours weekly. But this isn't just about logging more study hours. We've watched students discover what it means to truly submit to a discipline, to push beyond what's comfortable into what's transformative.

I think of Michael, who initially balked at the structure required for deep research. Yet as he delved into primary sources about World War II, something shifted. The discipline wasn't confining anymore. It had become a pathway to understanding. His personal fascination with military strategy blossomed into thoughtful discussions about leadership, courage, and the price of freedom.

What makes this phase uniquely powerful is how it weaves together personal growth and community engagement. Students begin to see their studies not just as personal achievements but as preparation for meaningful contributions. Natalia's passion for Shakespeare transformed into a student-led drama club for younger children. James' understanding of economics led him to help organize a community marketplace.

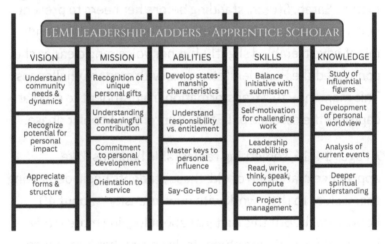

VISION	MISSION	ABILITIES	SKILLS	KNOWLEDGE
Understand community needs & dynamics	Recognition of unique personal gifts	Develop states-manship characteristics	Balance initiative with submission	Study of influential figures
Recognize potential for personal impact	Understanding of meaningful contribution	Understand responsibility vs. entitlement	Self-motivation for challenging work	Development of personal worldview
	Commitment to personal development	Master keys to personal influence	Leadership capabilities	Analysis of current events
Appreciate forms & structure	Orientation to service	Say-Go-Be-Do	Read, write, think, speak, compute	Deeper spiritual understanding
			Project management	

This is where the true magic happens. We've watched students grasp, often for the first time, how education can transform not just their own lives but their ability to influence the world around them. The discipline they're developing isn't just about academic success. It's preparation for the greater independence they'll experience as Self-Directed Scholars. Each essay written, each presentation given, each project completed, builds the internal structure they'll need for serious scholarship while keeping their sense of purpose alive and growing.

These Apprentice Scholar Ladders provide mentors with clear markers along this journey, while honoring each student's unique path. We're not creating cookie-cutter scholars. We're guiding individual hearts and minds toward their full potential. Students discover that true scholarship isn't just about personal achievement; it's about becoming someone who can make a difference in the world.

Self-Directed Scholar

Let me tell you about Leslie, a Self-Directed Scholar who took my breath away. At seventeen, she wasn't just studying the American Revolution – she was drawing unexpected connections between colonial resistance movements and modern grassroots organizing, all while leading a student-run historical preservation project in our community. Leslie was managing 60+ hours of weekly study, yet it never felt like "homework" to her. This was her passion, her purpose, her path.

This is the pinnacle of LEMI's Leadership Ladders – the Self-Directed Scholar phase, typically ages 16-18. These students aren't just independent learners; they're emerging scholars who have discovered their own intellectual hunger. They're not studying because someone told them to; they're pursuing knowledge because they can't imagine doing anything else.

I've watched students at this level wrestle with Plato late into the night, not because it was assigned, but because they couldn't stop thinking about his ideas. They don't just read the classics, they're transformed by them. Take Marcus, who found himself rethinking his entire approach to friendship after a deep dive into Aristotle's "Nicomachean Ethics."[7]

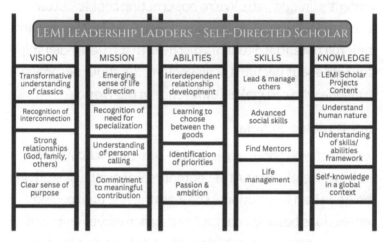

VISION	MISSION	ABILITIES	SKILLS	KNOWLEDGE
Transformative understanding of classics	Emerging sense of life direction	Interdependent relationship development	Lead & manage others	LEMI Scholar Projects Content
Recognition of interconnection	Recognition of need for specialization	Learning to choose between the goods	Advanced social skills	Understand human nature
Strong relationships (God, family, others)	Understanding of personal calling	Identification of priorities	Find Mentors	Understanding of skills/ abilities framework
Clear sense of purpose	Commitment to meaningful contribution	Passion & ambition	Life management	Self-knowledge in a global context

LEMI LEADERSHIP LADDERS – SELF-DIRECTED SCHOLAR

What makes this phase extraordinary is the beautiful balance students strike between independence and interconnection. They know when to work alone and when to seek guidance. They recognize that true scholarship isn't solitary. It's part of a greater conversation across time and disciplines. They're leading projects, organizing teams, and making real contributions to their communities, all while working closely with mentors and parents who help them refine their vision.

But here's where it gets really interesting. These students face choices that would challenge many adults. They're not just choosing between good and bad uses of their time; they're discerning between good, better, and best. Should they accept that internship or focus on their research project? Should they help launch a community initiative or dive deeper into their studies? These aren't easy decisions, but they're important ones.

As these young scholars prepare for their next phase – whether that's college, career, or specialized training – they're not just academically prepared. They're emerging as well-rounded individuals with a clear sense of purpose and the tools to pursue it. They're ready to engage expert mentors in their chosen fields while seeking that crucial depth of knowledge that marks true scholarship.

This is where we see Leadership Education in full bloom – young people who aren't just educated, but transformed, ready to dedicate more time to learning so they can make their unique mark on the world.

From Vision to Action

As we move forward in our exploration of Leadership Education, we turn our attention to the practical implementation of these foundational principles through key players and learning environments. Just as spiritual eyes and leadership ladders provide the framework for understanding student growth, the various players in the educational process—students, mentors, parents, content, and environments—work together to create the conditions where this growth can flourish. Next, we will explore how these elements combine to create what we call "The Learning Zone," where Leadership Education takes place.

Let's Take a Deeper Look – Chapter 3

These questions aren't just for pondering – they're invitations to connect these ideas with your own journey and vision as an educator. Take time to explore them deeply, perhaps journaling your thoughts or discussing them with fellow mentors.

1. Reflect on the Suzuki story where he spent time in darkness to understand how to teach a blind student. What does this teach us about developing spiritual eyes as mentors? How might you apply this level of empathetic understanding to your own mentoring?

2. Consider the Leadership Ladders (V-MASK – Vision, Mission, Abilities, Skills, Knowledge). Think of a student you're currently mentoring. Which ladder seems most relevant to their current challenges? How does identifying the specific ladder help you provide more targeted support?

3. The chapter describes the different phases of learning (Discovery, Practice Scholar, Apprentice Scholar, Self-Directed Scholar). Looking back on your own educational journey, how did you progress through these phases? How does understanding these phases change your approach to mentoring students at different stages?

4. Think about Enzio Busche's experience of facing the truth about himself. How does his story illuminate the

importance of self-honesty in both mentoring and learning? How might you create opportunities for students to develop this kind of self-awareness without the dramatic circumstances Busche faced?

5. The chapter emphasizes the importance of being still to see our students clearly. In our fast-paced educational environment, how might you create moments of stillness to better understand and serve your students? What practical steps could you take to develop your spiritual eyes?

Resources for Deeper Learning:

> **The Student Whisperer** by Oliver DeMille and Tiffany Earl[9]

> **"Language of Freedom" LEMIWorks! Podcast Episode,** a "Classic Call" episode. Found most major podcast platforms and LEMIWorks.com[10]

> **"Scholar Ladders" LEMIWorks! Podcast Episode**, a "Classic Call" episode. Found on most major podcast platforms and LEMIWorks.com.[11]

> **GRIT: The Power of Passion and Perseverance** by Angela Duckworth.[12]

CHAPTER 4

The Learning Zone &
Key Players of Leadership Education

Imagine a football game where one team knows only the ultimate goal—to get the ball across the finish line. They have no knowledge of rules, roles, positions, or boundaries. What would unfold on that field? Chaos. Disorganization. A lack of strategy, unity, and power. You'd see a jumble of individuals, all chasing the ball simultaneously, with no coordinated effort or plan to achieve their end goal.

Now, contrast this with a well-oiled sports team. What makes football, soccer, basketball, or any team sport truly work? It's the fact that every player knows their job. Each has a name, a role, and a purpose. They understand the guidelines of their respective positions and how to leverage their unique abilities.

The difference between good athletes on a competent team and those on a great team lies in their unity and interdependence. Great teams work together seamlessly because they trust the process, and each member takes full responsibility for their role. When every player knows their job and executes it well, magic happens on the field or court.

This same principle applies to the world of education—particularly when our goal is to cultivate leaders, statesmen, engaged citizens, and individuals who lead fulfilling,

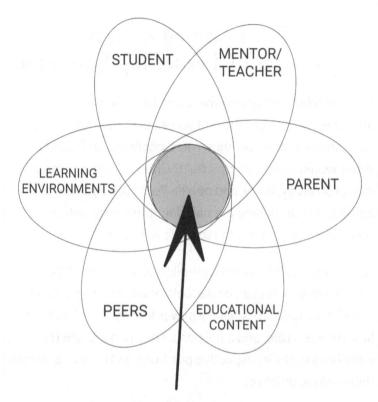

THE LEARNING ZONE

meaningful lives. Just as in sports, creating an environment where true learning and growth can occur requires a team of players, each with their own crucial role to play.

In the pages that follow, we'll introduce you to the key players on the Leadership Education team:

1. Student

2. Mentors and Teachers

3. Parents

4. Educational Content and Life Experience

5. Peers

6. Learning Environments

When all these players come together effectively, students naturally enter what we call the "Learning Zone"—a space where genuine learning, change, and growth occur organically.

By understanding each role and how they interact, we can create an educational experience that goes beyond mere information transfer. We can foster an environment that draws out each student's potential, encouraging them to take ownership of their learning journey and preparing them for a life of continuous growth and meaningful contribution.

Let's meet our team and discover how each player contributes to this educational approach.

The Student

In this team, the student is the central player. The student's role is fundamental yet profound: to be educable and teachable, to take ownership of their learning journey.

Education, at its core, means to "draw out" one's potential. This process can't be forced or coerced; it must come from within. As Shinichi Suzuki wisely noted, "One has to educate oneself from within to benefit from the greatness of others, only if one can do this can one fully realize the joy of being near someone who is great."[1]

True learning flourishes when it springs from within. Like a plant growing toward sunlight, students naturally stretch toward knowledge when three key elements align: the freedom to make meaningful choices about their learning path, the deep satisfaction that comes from conquering new challenges, and a compelling vision of why their learning matters. External motivators—whether carrots or sticks, gold stars or grades—pale in comparison to these powerful internal drives.

While mentors can illuminate the path and offer encouragement, they can't walk it for their students. Learning is an intimate journey that each person must undertake willingly. When students grasp this truth and step into their role as active architects of their own education rather than passive receivers of information, something remarkable happens. They tap into a wellspring of natural motivation that comes from truly owning their learning journey.

This shift—from being taught to truly learning—forms the bedrock of genuine education. It transforms students from passengers to pilots, from spectators to participants, igniting an internal spark that no external reward system could ever match.

The sooner students understand and embrace their role, the more fulfilling and effective their educational journey becomes. By taking responsibility for their own education, students not only acquire knowledge but also develop crucial life skills, such as self-motivation, critical thinking, and perseverance.

Key Responsibilities of the Student:

Throughout all phases of learning, students should maintain certain fundamental responsibilities that form the foundation of successful learning:

- Maintain a growth mindset and openness to learning.
- Take responsibility for their own learning journey.
- Practice regular self-reflection and adjustment.
- Build strong relationships with mentors and peers.
- Balance academic pursuits with personal well-being.
- Show respect for mentors and peers.
- Take ownership of mistakes and learn from them.
- Embrace challenges as opportunities for growth.

Discovery Phase Responsibilities (Ages 0-11)

From ages 0-11, children are developing character, emotional security, and foundational truths, while also engaging their natural curiosity and drive for exploration. During this time, students begin developing their role as active learners through age-appropriate responsibilities. They progress from simple tasks to more complex learning experiences, gradually building the habits and skills needed for scholarly work. Students master basic classroom routines, express needs appropriately, take initiative in areas of interest, and participate meaningfully in discussions. They learn to keep track of assignments, work cooperatively with peers, and begin developing basic study skills. This phase lays the groundwork for the more rigorous expectations of the Scholar Phase, with students progressively taking more responsibility for their learning while still receiving substantial guidance and support from mentors and parents.

Scholar Level Responsibilities (Ages 12-18)

As students progress into the Scholar Phase, their responsibilities expand to include scholar skills and more personal development. These responsibilities evolve through the Scholar sub-phases:

Practice Scholar (Ages 12-14)

- Begin developing independent study habits.
- Take ownership of daily schedule management.
- Participate actively in discussions and projects.
- Setting personal learning goals.
- Learn to balance different subjects and activities.
- Practice self-awareness
- Develop note-taking and organization systems.
- Begin using planners or time management tools.
- Become a person of action – "Don't just think of doing something, do it." [3]

Apprentice Scholar (Ages 14-16)

- Create and follow structured study schedules.
- Take full responsibility for completing assignments.
- Engage deeply in class discussions and debates.
- Set and track progress toward academic goals.
- Develop effective research skills.
- Practice critical thinking and analysis.
- Develop more emotional awareness and personal power to choose responses.

- Begin mentoring younger students.
- Maintain academic records and portfolios.

<u>Self-Directed Scholar (Ages 16-18)</u>

- Design and execute independent study plans.
- Manage projects and deadlines.
- Lead discussions and presentations.
- Seek out additional learning opportunities.
- Develop research capabilities.
- Apply knowledge across different subjects.
- Take initiative in pursuing areas of interest.
- Begin preparing for future academic/career goals.
- Engage mentors of their choosing.

By understanding and fulfilling these phase-appropriate responsibilities, students develop not just academic capabilities but also the character traits and skills essential for leadership and lifelong learning.

Remember, while these responsibilities become more complex with age, the fundamental principle remains constant – the student must be an active participant in their own education. No one else can do the learning for them, but with appropriate support and guidance, they can develop into capable, self-directed learners ready to make meaningful contributions to society. It's wise to remember that the students are real, live human beings who change from day to day, with good days and bad days, and the Scholar Phase, though it has high expectations, is also a place where mistakes can and should be made. It's a safe place to try hard things and fall flat on your face and then get back up again. It's not about being perfect at these lists; it is about learning and growing and getting better and better at learning to think, to write, to plan, to talk, to calculate, to feel, to express, to know how and when to make commitments, and to be patient.

(A sample Scholar Agreement is available on our website. See links at the end of the chapter.)

Mentors: The Guides on the Learning Journey

On the Leadership Education Team, mentors play a crucial role as guides, focusing primarily on the growth and development of the student. While teaching is an important aspect of education, true mentorship goes beyond imparting subject knowledge—it's about nurturing the whole person.

Effective mentors recognize patterns of growth and development in their students, particularly what we call the Liber Cycle (which we'll explore in detail shortly). When students encounter the "wall of ignorance" or face character challenges, mentors can:

- Remind students that these challenges are normal and necessary parts of growth.
- Share examples of their own journey through similar challenges.
- Help identify specific skills or abilities needed to overcome current obstacles.
- Provide encouragement and support without removing the growth opportunity.
- Celebrate transformations when students successfully

navigate challenges.

This understanding helps mentors distinguish between situations that require intervention and those where struggling is part of the learning process.

The Liber Cycle: A Framework for Growth

The Liber Cycle provides mentors with a framework to understand and navigate the challenges associated with learning and personal development. It describes a predictable pattern of growth that both mentors and students can use as a road map for achieving meaningful transformation.

Stages of the Liber Cycle:

1. <u>A True Principle</u> has been introduced, and the inspired student decides to apply it to their lives.

    For example, a student learns that it's his job to take responsibility for his education. It's not his mom's job or his dad's job. It's not the grocery clerk's job or his teacher's job. It's his. He courageously decides, "I am going to take full responsibility for what I do and don't learn."

2. <u>Honeymoon Phase:</u> This initial stage is characterized by high vision and excitement about newly discovered principles or possibilities along with low skills and abilities .

    To carry on with our example: The student is super excited that it's really up to him. If he understands the math assignment or doesn't understand it, it's up to him to find a way to understand it, or not to. No one else can be blamed. He feels excited about this true principle and the power it will bring into his life. He has no idea at this point that it might be difficult and hard. He is just happy to know he is the one in charge of his learning.

3. Application and Reality: As individuals begin to implement what they've learned, they often encounter difficulties and realize they lack certain skills or capabilities. This realization can be discouraging.

   The student scores poorly on a test and faces the reality that he alone is responsible for this result. Before, he might have blamed his teacher or maybe his little brother for keeping him up late. But now, he realizes he is personally responsible.

4. Persisting: Faced with challenges, individuals must choose between giving up (entering the "mediocrity loop") or persisting through difficulties.

   The student is tempted to blame his little brother for keeping him up last night and that's why he didn't do well on his test. But deep inside, he knows that he wasted several hours the day before when he could have been studying and reviewing the material. He chooses to take responsibility.

5. Character Challenge: Those who choose to persist face tests (external challenges), trials (unavoidable circumstances), and traps (internal weaknesses). This stage tests both ability and character.

   As the student continues to practice being fully responsible for his assignments, learning, and motivation to learn, he realizes he has some bad habits he had fallen into in the past. Through a conversation with his mentor,

The Learning Zone: Connecting Your Student's Heart, Mind & Purpose

they identified a familiar trap: believing math was boring. Because he is so accustomed to believing that "math is boring," this new understanding that this belief is a trap, and that he has the choice to stay in that trap or to pull himself out, is in and of itself liberating. Maybe math isn't boring. And what is truer is that concentrating and doing math is hard sometimes. And by using the past excuse that math is boring, he hasn't learned some key math concepts. He might have to go back and actually learn them. This could take an extra hour every day. This now is a trial he needs to simply get through; it's unavoidable. It will take persistence and continued belief in the principle that he is ultimately the one responsible for his education. Mentors can help identify and name common or specific traps. This awareness can be life changing for the student. The encouragement this student feels, to submit to actually learning the math that he had passed over, keeps him going, and he persists.

6. Transformation: Successfully working through challenges leads to transformation, resulting in increased capacity and tangible results.

After the student gets some math tutoring and gets through this year's math content, taking complete responsibility for his learning in math, he begins to recognize more quickly if he begins to make excuses in other areas. Having gone back and worked through this area of learning, he knew he didn't want to repeat that. He didn't want to deceive himself and make excuses. The student desires to be honest with himself from the get-go. This is game-changing, and he is better able to manage how much he wants to take on because he knows he is making a full commitment to it. He becomes wiser and more willing to back up and take things off his plate if necessary. This brings him peace.

7. <u>Live it:</u> This peace cannot be overstated. The growth that he has made by applying the truth that his role in education is to take responsibility for his education, then prepares him to learn the next principle and the next and the next. It lays the groundwork for further character development and for him to be the receptacle of virtue and truth.

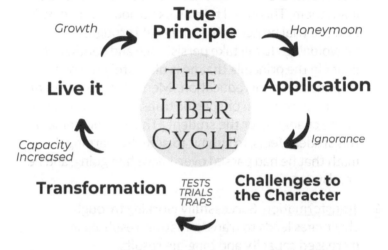

The Liber Cycle is the cycle of growth, we are always on it if we are growing. Sometimes detours take us away, but the decision to take responsibility for a true principle puts us back on it, and growth resumes.

Mentors as Guides

A mentor is like a seasoned explorer who has traversed the path of personal and intellectual growth. They use their experience and wisdom to guide students on their unique journeys. Unlike a traditional teacher who might focus solely on curriculum, a mentor meets students at their developmental level.

The Mentor's Core Responsibilities

Using Spiritual Eyes
Identify your student's next step up the Leadership Ladders of Vision, Mission, Abilities, Skills, and Knowledge

Seeing The Bigger Picture
Understanding educational phases as well as your student and their potential.

Live the Liber Cycle
Harness personal growth and inspire and guide your student's growth

The Mentor

Understand Agency
Mentors teach, inspire, guide, and hold accountable. Students are not forced to learn, they have agency. It's up to them to be educable.

Be a Team Player
Effectively use the Leadership Team to draw out your student's potential

The mentor's role centers on five fundamental responsibilities that remain constant throughout all phases of learning, though their practical application naturally adjusts to match the student's developmental stage and needs:

- **Seeing the Bigger Picture:** Understanding each student's developmental journey and recognizing how current experiences connect to future growth.
- **Live the Liber Cycle:** Experiencing and modeling the process of growth through applying true principles,

The Learning Zone & Key Players of Leadership Education

facing challenges, and achieving transformation.

- **Be a Team Player:** Working effectively with parents, other mentors, and the broader educational community to support student development.
- **Understand Agency:** Respecting and supporting students' capacity for choice while providing appropriate guidance and boundaries.
- **Using Spiritual Eyes:** Perceiving each student's unique gifts, challenges, and possibilities while discerning their next right steps for growth.

The Shift from Teaching to Mentoring

We aspire for all educators to embrace the role of mentor. This means going beyond the traditional teacher-student dynamic to create a more personalized approach to education. Mentors prioritize the student's overall growth over mere information transfer, recognizing that true education encompasses far more than academic knowledge. They develop a deep understanding of each student's unique potential, challenges, and aspirations, allowing them to provide targeted guidance and support. Central to this approach is the cultivation of a relationship based on trust, respect, and mutual learning, where both mentor and student grow through their interactions. Mentors use their spiritual eyes to meet each student's individual needs and learning styles, recognizing that one size does not fit all in education. Perhaps most importantly, they encourage self-discovery and self-directed learning, empowering students to take ownership of their educational journey and become lifelong learners. In this way, mentors don't just teach subjects; they guide individuals toward realizing their full potential and finding their unique path in life. One way to understand it is that the mentor's subject is the student. Every time they give feedback and correction or guidance, they have that student's soul in the palms of their hands.

Core Responsibilities of Mentors Across All Phases

Before exploring phase-specific responsibilities, certain fundamental duties remain constant for mentors:

- Model lifelong learning and personal growth.
- Maintain unwavering belief in each student's potential..
- Create safe, nurturing learning environments .
- Adapt learning environments and assignments to meet individual needs .
- Stay current with Leadership Education principles.
- Maintain clear communication with parents.
- Continue personal development.
- Use your Spiritual Eyes to discern the student's next steps and needs.

Discovery Phase Mentor Responsibilities (Ages 0-12)

During the Discovery Phase, mentors focus on awakening wonder and establishing foundational learning habits. They must be attuned to developmental readiness, recognizing each child's unique pace.

Key responsibilities include:

- Design engaging, hands-on learning experiences.
- Observe and document student learning patterns.
- Guide development of basic study skills through work and play.

- Foster positive associations with learning.
- Develop emotional awareness and social skills.
- Create age-appropriate leadership opportunities.
- Support transition to formal learning (Ages 6-12).
- Partner with parents for consistent support.

Scholar Phase Mentor Responsibilities (Ages 12-18)

During the Scholar Phase, mentor responsibilities evolve through three distinct sub-phases, each building upon the previous while introducing new levels of complexity and independence. Let's examine the specific responsibilities for each sub-phase:

Practice Scholar Phase (Ages 12-14)
- Guide development of basic scholarly habits.
- Help structure discretionary time (15-25 hours weekly).
- Introduce critical thinking principles, forms, and pattern recognition of behaviors and actions.
- Support independence within clear boundaries.
- Foster positive peer relationships.
- Develop basic research and writing skills.
- Guide discovery of interests.
- Establish study routines.
- Encourage regular self-awareness patterns.

Apprentice Scholar Phase (Ages 14-16)

- Set rigorous academic expectations.
- Support increased study time (up to 40 hours weekly).
- Guide engagement with classic texts.
- Develop advanced research and writing skills.
- Foster ability to discuss, continuing to dialogue about forms.

- Support emerging leadership.
- Guide time management development.
- Encourage personal responsibility over choices.

Self-Directed Scholar Phase (Ages 16-18)

- Support independent study initiatives.
- Guide extensive study time (40-80 hours weekly).
- Facilitate advanced research.
- Prepare for future academic pursuits.
- Foster high-level analysis and synthesis.
- Guide original thinking development.
- Foster discussions of complex ideas about forms, learning to distinguish between issues and principles, action and results, propaganda and what is real.
- Support scholarly voice emergence.
- Facilitate transition to adult learning.

The Art of Using Your Spiritual Eyes

Successful mentoring requires moments of stillness, where mentors cultivate their capacity to see beyond the surface and discern their students' deeper needs. Through developing their spiritual eyes, mentors learn to recognize when students are ready for new challenges and identify which leadership ladder might be blocking their progress. This perceptive awareness allows mentors to skillfully adjust their support levels, providing just enough guidance while maintaining appropriately high standards. By staying attuned to each student's unique journey, mentors can strike the delicate balance between academic rigor and emotional support, fostering independence while ensuring students have the scaffolding they need to succeed. This careful attention to both the visible and invisible aspects of student development creates an environment where genuine growth can flourish.

Fostering Intrinsic Motivation

Mentors guide students from external to internal motivation through careful observation and patience.

The LEMI Scholar Projects demonstrate this progression through carefully designed transitions in motivation and reward. Practice Scholar projects begin by incorporating meaningful external rewards, such as ceremonial swords and coronation ceremonies, which help spark initial engagement. As students advance to Apprentice Scholar projects, the focus naturally shifts toward intrinsic rewards, with students finding satisfaction in mastery demonstration and intellectual discourse. Through this thoughtful progression, the ultimate goal emerges: helping students discover deep personal satisfaction in their own growth and meaningful contribution to the world around them.

Remember, mentoring requires wisdom, patience, and constant refinement. Likewise, mentors prepare students not just for immediate success but for lifelong learning and leadership.

(A sample Mentor Agreement is available on our website. See links at the end of the chapter.)

Parents: The Foundational Influencers

In Leadership Education, parents are key players on the

educational team, not outside observers. Their active engagement is essential, whether in homeschooling, the Leadership Education community, or formal school settings.

Parents are the most constant and influential presence in a child's life. No one knows the child better or has a stronger vested interest in their success. This philosophy explicitly rejects the "drop-off" mentality where parents delegate educational responsibility entirely to teachers or schools.

Primary Responsibilities:

Knowing Their Child

Parents must develop a deep understanding of their child's personality, interests, strengths, and challenges. This involves carefully observing learning patterns and behavior while staying attuned to signs of readiness for new challenges. Through this careful attention, parents become skilled at identifying their child's emotional and social needs, creating a foundation for effective support and guidance.

Believing in Their Child

A parent's unwavering support through challenges forms the bedrock of a child's confidence and growth. This involves consistently seeing and nurturing potential, while supporting appropriate risk-taking that allows children to stretch and develop. Parents demonstrate this belief by celebrating genuine progress, recognizing that each step forward contributes to their child's development.

Loving and Nurturing

Parents create an environment of emotional security that allows children to thrive. By establishing a supportive home environment, they foster confidence and resilience in their children. This nurturing approach includes maintaining unconditional positive regard, ensuring children feel valued and supported regardless of circumstances.

Facilitating Growth

Parents actively create learning opportunities that align with their child's interests and developmental needs. This includes supporting dedicated study time and space, ensuring necessary resources are available, and connecting children with appropriate mentors who can guide specific areas of development.

Collaborating with Mentors

Effective collaboration requires maintaining regular communication with mentors while actively supporting educational goals at home. Parents enhance this partnership by participating in parent education opportunities and contributing to the broader learning community, creating a unified support system for their child's growth.

Holding Parent Mentor Meetings

Regular parent mentor meetings provide essential structure for supporting student growth. During these meetings, parents assist in setting appropriate goals and targets while cultivating trust and openness. These sessions provide space to work through struggles, hold the student accountable, and create a reliable place for reporting back on progress and challenges.

Implementation Across Settings

Homeschool:

- Serve as primary mentors
- Create structured learning environments
- Coordinate with outside mentors
- Participate in homeschool communities

Leadership Education Communities:

- Participate in community events
- Support other families
- Share resources
- Attend parent education

Traditional School:

- Stay informed about the curriculum
- Support learning at home
- Maintain contact with teachers
- Create a supportive home environment

Parent Mentor Meetings

Regular one-on-one meetings with each child provide essential opportunities for growth and connection. Through these meetings, children develop integrity by making and following through on commitments while engaging in meaningful goal setting and review. Students build crucial task management skills and find a safe space for expressing their thoughts and feelings. These meetings consistently reinforce that the students are heard and respected, creating a foundation of trust and open communication.

Continuous Parent Development

Effective parental involvement requires ongoing personal growth and education. Parents enhance their effectiveness through training in Leadership Education Principles and active participation in parent education opportunities. They strengthen their support network by building connections with other parents and mentors while continuing their own personal education journey. This commitment to continuous learning models the lifelong learning mindset essential to Leadership Education.

Parents are active partners in education, working with mentors to create rich, supportive learning environments. Their engagement contributes to both academic success and overall development of confident, capable individuals prepared for lifelong learning and leadership.

(A sample Parent Agreement is available on our website. See links at the end of the chapter.)

Educational Content and Life Experiences: Choosing Wisely

In Leadership Education, the selection of material and content is crucial. As Joshua Cooper Ramo insightfully noted, "We are what we are connected to."[2] This principle applies not just to our social networks but also to the intellectual content we engage with. The books we read, the ideas we ponder, and the classics we study shape our thinking, our character, and ultimately, our potential for leadership.

The Power of Wise Selection

While the world offers infinite learning possibilities, not all content is created equal. We emphasize:

1. **Quality over Quantity:** It's not about exposing students to every piece of information, but rather providing them with rich, thought-provoking material that ignites a passion for learning, for understanding human nature, and is a launching pad for growth.

2. **Depth over Breadth**: Deep exploration of subjects gives students the skills and desire to take a deep dive into any topic that interests them. For example, a thorough study of Shakespeare's works or Virgil's Georgics can provide students with the tools to approach any complex text or idea.

3. **Wholesome Content:** While acknowledging the existence of both good and evil in the world, we prioritize material that uplifts, expands the heart, and inspires the mind. If we must choose between good and evil, we choose good. If we must choose between good, better, and best, we choose best. This doesn't mean that great works that show the results of evil or mediocrity aren't included. They are.

4. **The Great Conversation:** We encourage students to engage with the ongoing dialogue that philosophers, scientists, and thinkers have been having throughout history about life's big questions. This includes works

that promote critical thinking about happiness, the purpose of life, and how to find meaning.

Examples of Powerful Content

1. **The Simple Yet Profound:** Consider William Bentley, who spent fifty years studying snowflakes. His dedication to this "simple" subject led him to become proficient in multiple disciplines, including artistry, science, writing, speaking, and photography. His work demonstrates how deep engagement with even a seemingly basic topic can lead to multifaceted learning and discovery.[4]

2. **The Complex and Timeless:** On the other end of the spectrum, we have works like Shakespeare's sonnets, plays, and poems. These complex pieces of literature have been studied for centuries, continually offering new insights into language, human nature, and the human condition.

3. **The Inspirational:** Works that fill the soul, expand the heart, and inspire the mind are particularly valuable. This could include biographies of great leaders, philosophical treatises on ethics, or scientific works that reveal the wonders of the natural world.

4. **The Challenging:** Content that pushes students out of their comfort zones and challenges their assumptions can be incredibly valuable. This might include works from different cultures or time periods that present unfamiliar worldviews.

The Buffet Analogy

Choosing content wisely is like curating a rich educational buffet. We don't want to limit students to the "cheese and crackers" of education, just learning the basic skills like math, reading, and writing. Instead, we want them to have these skills so they can feast on "fruits and vegetables, wines and cheese." We want them to read Plato, listen to Bach, walk the shores of Galilee (metaphorically or literally), and attend performances of Les Misérables.[5]

Empowering Self-Education

The ultimate goal in choosing material and content is not to disseminate all knowledge but to inspire students to become lifelong learners. We aim to:

1. Give students a vision of what's possible through exposure to great ideas and achievements.

2. Equip them with the skills to manage their time, read critically, and write effectively.

3. Instill a hunger for continuous learning and self-improvement.

4. Inspire a deep sense of awareness and stillness so that truths can be distilled upon the mind and heart.

5. Teach them how to think.

By carefully selecting and presenting rich, diverse, and challenging content, we prepare students not just for academic success but for a lifetime of learning, growth, and meaningful contribution to the world.

Remember, we are what we connect to. By connecting students to the best that has been thought and said throughout human history, we're setting them on a path to becoming the best versions of themselves.

Peers: Creating Dynamic Learning Communities

Like a theatrical production where supporting actors enhance the lead performer's role, peers play a vital part on the Leadership Education team. While students, mentors, parents, and content form the foundation, peers—including siblings, friends, family, and classmates—create the dynamic learning community where principles can be practiced and leadership skills developed.

Just as choosing the right content and material matters, so does choosing a child's peers. Not all material is equal, and timing matters when it comes to introducing material. It is the same for choosing peers. We become like those we spend time with. This means cultivating communities and friendships where there is a shared culture and vision of what is important.

Core Contributions Across Phases

Discovery Phase (Ages 0-11)

During this crucial period of character development and competence peers provide:

- Practical playmates
- Opportunities to work together and play together.
- Real life situations to learn character traits such as forgiveness, kindness, gentleness, meekness, and personal awareness.

- Practice developing communication and listening skills.
- Friendships
- Development of emotional skills such as modulating and normalizing as extroverted and introverted children learn to go from group activities to individual activities.

Scholar Phase (Ages 12 and Up)

For scholar phase students, peers whose families ideally share the values and vision of a Leadership Education become indispensable. Many learning environments require group interaction, complementing individual study and one-on-one mentoring. Through peer interactions, students:

- Explore and share insights and ideas, learning to voice their own thoughts and feelings as well as seek to understand someone else's ideas.
- Work together in creating finished products: theater, dances, sports, music, etc.
- Develop meaningful relationships.
- Gain personal awareness as they learn to gently and appropriately express emotions and thoughts.
- Grow in a variety of abilities such as: patience, kindness, forgiveness, generosity, abundance mentality, fortitude, and charity.
- Have a safe place to make mistakes together as they all grow.
- Practice receiving feedback from others.
- Are challenged in their ability to reason and express.
- Refine their etiquette.
- Give service.
- Get practice teaching others.
- Share excitement about what they love.
- Explore new ideas and places that their peers bring to the table.

The Learning Zone & Key Players of Leadership Education

The Impact of Peer Relationships

We can see that peers help an individual have an opportunity for more growth. They help the student crystallize ideas and feelings. They make it possible to work in groups, allowing collaboration and fostering creativity. Peers also allow a student to be challenged emotionally as well as academically. And peers can be really inspiring. Seeing good choices that others make can inspire the student, and seeing bad choices that others make can also help a student stop and think about what choices they themselves are making.

Creating Supportive Peer Communities

This is why ideally, Leadership Education is a family affair. Finding other like-minded families and mentors, who believe education is about fostering environments that will help the child grow in character as well as in competence in a myriad of areas, and who respect a child's agency as well as understanding their growth, really matters. Encouraging your child and your student to become the type of friend and peer you both hope they can find is a great way to help students understand their role as a Peer themselves.

The Power of Integration

Like a well-practiced team, the key players in Leadership Education—Students, Mentors, Parents, and Educational Content—must work in harmony. Each player's understanding of their role and how it complements others creates the foundation for effective learning.

The Learning Zone: Connecting Your Student's Heart, Mind & Purpose

Yet, our exploration isn't complete without examining the sixth crucial element: The Learning Environments. Just as concert hall acoustics affect a musician's performance, the environment where learning occurs shapes educational outcomes. A history lesson that seems dry in a classroom might spark excitement during a historical reenactment.

These six elements—Students, Mentors and Teachers, Parents,Educational Content and Life Experience, Peers, and Learning Environments—form an interconnected system where each component influences the others. As we explore the Learning Environments in detail, we'll discover how each one, when thoughtfully implemented, amplifies the effectiveness of the entire educational process. Understanding the unique characteristics and potential of each environment will help us create more engaging, meaningful, and transformative educational experiences.

Just as great teams thrive within supportive communities— from enthusiastic fans to dedicated support staff— Leadership Education flourishes when embedded in nurturing communities. These communities provide crucial support networks for families and students alike. They create environments where learning can take root and grow, where parents can find encouragement and guidance, and where students can develop alongside peers who share their values and aspirations. Like a home team's community that rallies behind their players, these communities unite around shared principles and goals, fostering an atmosphere where each player can excel in their role.

With our understanding of these key players and their roles firmly established, we turn now to explore the learning environments themselves. These carefully crafted spaces and experiences, when thoughtfully implemented, create the conditions where our educational team can achieve its highest potential. In Chapter 5, we'll examine how these learning environments—ranging from dynamic discussions to focused simulations—work together to develop both competence and character in tomorrow's leaders.

Let's Take a Deeper Look – Chapter 4

These questions aren't just for pondering – they're invitations to connect these ideas with your own journey and vision as an educator. Take time to explore them deeply, perhaps journaling your thoughts or discussing them with fellow mentors.

1. Do your students fully understand their role? If they learn to take responsibility for their learning how will this change your classroom?

2. Understanding Your Responsibilities: Given your role, what specific responsibilities do you have in ensuring that the educational content you select or engage with is of high quality and aligns with the principles of Leadership Education? How can you contribute to the "buffet" of rich, diverse, and challenging content?

3. Collaborating for Optimal Learning: How can you effectively collaborate with others in the educational ecosystem (students, mentors, parents, content creators) to create a more transformative and enriching learning experience? What steps can you take to ensure that everyone is "on the same page" when it comes to selecting and utilizing powerful, transformative content?

4. Personal Growth Through Content: Reflecting on Joshua Cooper Ramo's quote, "We are what we are connected to," how has your own intellectual and

personal growth been shaped by the content you've engaged with? How can you be more intentional about your "connections" to educational material moving forward?

Resources for Deeper Learning:

Example Scholar, Mentor, and Parent contracts are available for free download on our book web page - **LEMI-U.com/Learning-Zone**

Drive: The Surprising Truth About What Motivates Us by Daniel Pink[6]

The Mentor's Handbook by Aneladee Milne[7] (available at LEMIHomeschool.com)

CHAPTER 5

Learning Environments:
An Element of
Leadership Education

Imagine a scenario where students are genuinely excited to learn, eagerly seeking more knowledge, and willingly investing time in the challenging tasks of thinking, reading, and writing. This isn't a utopian dream—it's the potential reality that well-crafted learning environments can create.

Consider the experience of Amy Bowler, a mentor teaching a QUEST class (an apprentice scholar project focusing on principles, personal development, and leadership training). When she noticed her students struggling to engage in discussions about Gandhi, she took an innovative approach to transform the learning environment. Amy brought homemade Indian food to class, removed the tables, and had everyone sit on blankets while listening to Indian music. This simple yet thoughtful change in the physical and sensory environment sparked vibrant discussions and deepened the students' connection to the subject matter. Her creative approach demonstrates how even small changes to the learning environment can have a significant impact on student engagement and learning outcomes.[1]

While Amy's creative use of the physical space helped enhance her students' engagement, it's important to understand that when we discuss "Learning Environments" in Leadership Education, we're not primarily talking about physical spaces. Rather, we're referring to distinct approaches or methods through which learning occurs—such as discussions, simulations, or tutorials. These environments are more about how we structure and facilitate learning experiences than about where they take place. Though physical settings can certainly support these environments, as Amy's example shows, it's the intentional design of the learning experience itself that defines each environment.

In the intricate tapestry of Leadership Education, learning environments stand as the sixth essential element, joining Students, Mentors and Teachers, Parents, Educational Content, and Peers in shaping educational experiences. Far from being a mere backdrop, the learning environment actively participates in the educational process by:

- Sparking and maintaining student interest in the material
- Fostering emotional connections to the content
- Enhancing comprehension and retention of knowledge
- Encouraging critical thinking and self-expression

When implemented thoughtfully, these environments transform classrooms, homes, and workshops into safe spaces where students can explore their thoughts and feelings about the material and their relationship to it. Our goal is to empower educators to seamlessly integrate these environments into their daily teaching practices, creating rich, varied, and engaging learning experiences.

Indicators of Effective Learning Environments

An effective learning environment is one where students feel safe to express themselves fully. Ask yourself: In this environment, do my students feel free to...?:

- Laugh
- Cry
- Sigh
- Dance
- Groan
- Share their feelings and thoughts

If the answer is yes, you've created a space where curiosity can flourish, and natural learning and growth can occur.

How Learning Environments Work Together

Each learning environment brings unique strengths that enhance and reinforce the others:

- Example sets the foundation for all learning, showing students what's possible.
- Discussions and colloquia bring ideas to life through collaborative exploration.
- Reading and writing develop deep understanding and clear expression.
- Tutorials and coaching provide personalized guidance for growth.
- Lectures inspire and inform while building shared knowledge.
- Simulations bridge theory and practice through

experiential learning.

- Testing, Performance, and Teaching become tools for self-discovery rather than mere assessment.
- Debriefing transforms all these experiences into lasting wisdom.

Principles for Effective Implementation

Success in creating powerful learning environments rests on several key principles:

1. Clear Learning Objectives

- Define specific goals for each learning session: Your know, feel, do
- Consider both immediate and long-term outcomes
- Align environmental choices with desired results

2. Strategic Selection

- Choose environments that best serve your objectives
- Consider student readiness and capabilities
- Account for available resources and constraints

3. Thoughtful Integration

- Create meaningful sequences of learning experiences
- Build connections between different environments
- Allow insights from one environment to enhance others

4. Responsive Adaptation

- Monitor student engagement and comprehension
- Watch for signs of confusion or disconnection
- Make real-time adjustments based on feedback

Flexibility in Practice

The art of orchestrating learning environments lies in remaining responsive to student needs while maintaining clear educational objectives. Consider these possible scenarios for combining environments effectively:

When Students Struggle with Concepts:

1. Begin with Example to demonstrate understanding

2. Move to Tutorial for personalized guidance

3. Use Discussion to explore different perspectives

4. Conclude with Writing to solidify understanding

When Exploring New Topics:

1. Start with Lecture to provide context or an introduction

2. Follow with Reading for deeper exploration

3. Use Discussion to process insights

4. Apply learning through Simulation

5. Conclude with Debrief to integrate understanding

When Building Skills:

1. Begin with Example to show mastery

2. Provide Tutorial or Lecture with vision casting for specific techniques

3. Use Coaching to address individual challenges

4. Implement Testing to gauge progress

5. End with Debrief to plan next steps

Looking Forward

Among the learning environments we've explored, Example stands as the foundation upon which all others build. Just as Amy Bowler's creative approach to teaching Gandhi demonstrated the power of thoughtful environmental design, a mentor's example shapes every aspect of the learning experience. Whether leading discussions, guiding reading selections, or facilitating simulations, the mentor's modeling of curiosity, critical thinking, and character creates an invisible yet powerful learning environment that operates continuously.

In our next chapter, we'll explore how Example functions as both our first and most pervasive learning environment. We'll examine how a mentor's example inspires growth, demonstrates principles in action, and creates an atmosphere where genuine learning flourishes. Through this exploration, we'll discover that being an exemplary mentor isn't about perfection but about authentic engagement with our own growth journey—a journey that invites students to embark on their own paths of discovery and development.

Let's Take a Deeper Look — Chapter 5

The Learning Zone: Connecting Your Student's Heart, Mind & Purpose

These questions aren't just for pondering – they're invitations to connect these ideas with your own journey and vision as an educator. Take time to explore them deeply, perhaps journaling your thoughts or discussing them with fellow mentors.

1. Can you think of a specific instance where the environment significantly impacted your learning, either positively or negatively?

2. This chapter suggests that effective learning environments allow students to express themselves freely (laugh, cry, sigh, etc.). How might creating this type of safe environment change the dynamics of learning?

3. Think about the ten learning environments listed in the chapter. Which of these do you feel most comfortable with as a learner or educator? Which ones challenge you the most? How might you work to become more proficient in the environments you find challenging?

Resources for Deeper Learning:

LEMI Essential Foundations Online Course - free and available on LEMI-U.com[2]

Family Foundations Subscription – An online course that inspires and supports parents in doing the most important work we will ever do - fulfilling our missions within our homes! Available on LEMIHomeschool.com [3]

CHAPTER 6

The Power of Example:
Mentorship Beyond Words

Imagine a classroom without walls, where learning flows
through every interaction, every decision, and every
moment shared between mentor and student. Like ripples
spreading across a pond, a mentor's actions and attitudes
create waves of influence that shape not just what students
learn, but how they approach life itself. This invisible
classroom, created through the power of example,
transcends traditional educational settings and permeates
every aspect of the mentor-student relationship.

The Power of Example

The most profound teaching often happens not through
formal instruction but through the quiet power of example.
When mentors embody the qualities and skills they hope to
instill, they create a living curriculum more compelling than
any textbook. This environmental approach to mentorship
transforms every interaction into an opportunity for growth
and learning. The way the mentor lives their life creates the
authority by which they mentor.

Consider Sarah, a science mentor who regularly brings her
own research journals to class. When students see her
excitement as she shares new discoveries or admits
uncertainty about conflicting data, they learn more than just

scientific facts. They absorb essential lessons about intellectual curiosity, academic honesty, and the joy of discovery. Through Sarah's example, students learn that science is not just a subject to study but a way of engaging with the world.

Think about a child learning to talk. The example of their parents, siblings, and playmates gets them babbling. If I were to guess, less than ten percent of a child learning to talk is through anything other than example. It happens naturally and without formality. Yet it is one of the richest environments. Example is louder than words. Do as I do is so much more powerful than do as I say while ignoring what I do.

The Learning Zone: Connecting Your Student's Heart, Mind & Purpose

Key Areas of Influence

Living Curriculum Through Daily Actions

When mentors consciously align their actions with their teaching, they create powerful learning opportunities in several crucial areas:

Lifelong Learning and Intellectual Curiosity

Mentors demonstrate their commitment to learning by actively pursuing new knowledge and skills while sharing their discoveries and insights with genuine enthusiasm. They thoughtfully embrace new technologies and methodologies, using wisdom to discern their appropriate application. Through demonstrating a genuine passion for learning and consistently encouraging questions and exploration, they inspire students to develop their own love of discovery and growth.

Critical Thinking and Analysis

Effective mentors model analytical skills by demonstrating their ability to challenge assumptions and thoughtfully evaluate information. They engage in respectful debate that showcases how to navigate differing viewpoints productively. Through teaching with real-world examples and consistently modeling analytical processes, they help students develop their own critical thinking capabilities and understand how to apply these skills in meaningful ways.

Resilience and Growth Mindset

By sharing personal stories of overcoming challenges and

deliberately framing failures as valuable learning opportunities, mentors help students develop resilience. They demonstrate persistence toward goals while approaching difficulties with consistent optimism. Through showing how setbacks can become stepping stones to success, they help students develop the resilience and growth mindset essential for long-term achievement.

Emotional Intelligence

A mentor's emotional intelligence shapes the learning environment in profound ways, establishing patterns that students often carry forward into their own lives and leadership roles:

Self-Awareness and Regulation

Mentors demonstrate emotional intelligence by openly acknowledging their own emotional states and modeling constructive ways to process feelings. They take intentional time to reflect and reframe situations, showing appropriate vulnerability when sharing their own growth journey. Through making mindful choices under pressure, they demonstrate how to maintain composure and thoughtful decision-making even in challenging circumstances.

Empathy and Connection

Through their interactions, mentors teach students the essential skills of listening actively and deeply to others while validating their experiences. They model how to recognize emotional cues and navigate challenging conversations with sensitivity and respect. By demonstrating these skills consistently, mentors show students how to build meaningful relationships that foster both personal growth and mutual understanding.

These emotional capabilities become particularly powerful when mentors create structured opportunities for students to practice them through:

- Guided reflection exercises
- Group discussions about emotional experiences
- Feedback exchanges
- Conflict resolution practice
- Team-building activities

The Journey Forward

The journey of exemplary mentorship is not about achieving perfection but about demonstrating authentic growth. Effective mentors:

- Embrace their own learning journey
- Seek regular feedback
- Engage in continuous professional development
- Practice self-reflection and goal-setting
- Model resilience through challenges
- Embrace the seasons of their life

When mentors openly share their growth process while maintaining professional boundaries, they show students that development is lifelong and that leadership requires continuous learning.

Consider Michael, a writing mentor who regularly shares

drafts of his own work with students. By showing them his revision process, including moments of uncertainty and breakthrough, he demonstrates that mastery comes through practice and persistence. His vulnerability in sharing unfinished work creates an environment where students feel safe to take creative risks and learn from mistakes.

Creating Lasting Impact

The power of example creates ripples that extend far beyond the immediate learning environment. Through conscious modeling of curiosity, resilience, emotional intelligence, and continuous growth, mentors establish patterns that can influence students' lives for years to come.

As the ancient Chinese philosopher Lao Tzu is said to have observed, when the best leaders have completed their work, the people believe they have accomplished it themselves.[1] This wisdom captures the essence of mentorship through example. By creating an environment rich in living examples of leadership and learning, mentors empower students to discover their own potential and embark on their unique journeys of growth.

While the power of example provides an essential foundation, students need opportunities to engage with and process what they observe. This brings us to our next learning environment: group discussions and colloquia. Through thoughtful dialogue and collaborative exploration, students begin to articulate their understanding, challenge their assumptions, and build upon the principles they've witnessed in their mentors. As we'll explore in the next chapter, these discussions create dynamic spaces where individual observations transform into collective wisdom through the power of shared inquiry.

Let's Take a Deeper Look — Chapter 6

These questions aren't just for pondering – they're invitations to connect these ideas with your own journey and vision as an educator. Take time to explore them deeply, perhaps journaling your thoughts or discussing them with fellow mentors.

1. Think about a mentor who has had a significant impact on your life. What specific examples did they set that influenced you? How did their actions, rather than just their words, shape your growth?

2. In your current role as a mentor or educator, what are three specific ways you can better model the qualities you want to instill in your students or mentees?

3. Reflect on your own journey of personal and professional growth. How can you make this process more visible to those you mentor, demonstrating the value of lifelong learning?

4. Think about a time when you made a mistake or faced a significant challenge in front of your mentees. How did you handle it? How could you use such situations to model resilience and a growth mindset?

Resources for Deeper Learning:

Family Foundations Subscription – An online course that inspires and supports parents in doing the most important work we will ever do - fulfilling our missions within our homes! Available on LEMIHomeschool.com [2]

A House United: Changing Children's Hearts and Behaviors by Teaching Self-Government by Nicholeen Peck[3]

Revolutionary Families Podcast with Kent & Amy Bowler[4]

Mindset: The New Psychology of Success by Carol Dweck[5]

CHAPTER 7

Group Discussion/Colloquia: The Art of Educere — To Draw Out

Sarah watched as her normally quiet student, David, suddenly leaned forward, eyes bright with enthusiasm. "But what if Thoreau wasn't just writing about living in the woods?" he exclaimed. "What if Walden Pond was really about finding yourself by stepping away from society's expectations?" [1]

Emma, another student who rarely spoke up in regular classes, built on David's insight. "That connects to what we read in Plato's Cave – about breaking free from illusions and seeing reality clearly for the first time." [2]

The energy in the room was electric as more students joined in, drawing unexpected connections between texts they'd read throughout the semester. Even Michael, who typically stared at his phone during traditional lectures, was fully engaged, scribbling notes as his peers shared insights he'd never considered.

Sarah smiled, remembering her own uncertainty when she first began leading discussions. Now she understood that magic happens when students feel safe enough to think aloud together, to test ideas and build on each others insights. This wasn't just students talking – it was collaborative discovery in action, transforming passive learners into active seekers of wisdom.

In Leadership Education, discussions and colloquia serve as powerful tools for developing critical thinking and deeper understanding. This takes two primary forms: group discussions and colloquia, each serving distinct but complementary purposes in the learning journey.

Group discussions provide a more informal, flexible environment where students can explore ideas, solve problems, and build confidence in sharing their thoughts. These sessions, which might emerge spontaneously from classroom activities or be loosely structured around current topics, allow for dynamic interaction and help students develop basic analytical skills. The teacher or mentor typically takes an active role in facilitating these discussions, guiding students through their initial exploration of ideas.

Colloquia, in contrast, offers a more formal and structured setting. These carefully planned sessions typically last between 1-2 hours and involve 6 to 30 participants. They center on classic texts or significant works that participants have studied in advance. In a colloquium, the mentor's role is that of a guide, helping students engage in deep analysis and philosophical exploration. Through an emphasis on connecting ideas across texts and disciplines, colloquia challenges students to gain insights and understanding. Colloquia can be guided by one mentor or two, where the two mentors work in tandem to create rich discussion and dialogue.

Group Discussions vs. Colloquia

Aspect	Group Discussions	Colloquia
Format	More informal and flexible	More formal and structured
Size	Variable group size	6-30 participants
Duration	Flexible timing	Usually 1-2 hours
Preparation	Minimal to moderate preparation	Extensive preparation required
Content	Current topics, spontaneous subjects	Classic texts or significant works
Mentor Role	Active facilitator, guides conversation	Guide and observer, less direct involvement
Structure	Looser format, allows tangents	Clear format with specific protocols
Purpose	Explore ideas, solve problems, build confidence	Deep analysis, philosophical exploration
Student Role	Active participants, sharing thoughts	Scholars engaged in deep analysis
Depth	Basic to intermediate analysis	Advanced analysis and synthesis
Focus	Building basic analytical skills	Connecting ideas across texts and disciplines
Outcomes	Initial understanding and engagement	Transformative insights, deeper understanding

Both formats play pivotal roles in Leadership Education, offering students opportunities to expand their perspectives, clarify their thoughts, and discover personal insights. The choice between group discussion and colloquium depends on factors such as the students' developmental stage, the complexity of the material, and the specific learning objectives. Together, these complementary approaches create a robust framework for developing critical thinking and analytical abilities.

Now that we've established the distinct roles of group discussions and colloquia let's delve deeper into the mechanics of facilitating effective group discussions. Understanding the structure and key elements of these sessions is crucial for mentors and educators looking to maximize their impact on student learning and engagement.

Understanding how to effectively use group discussions and colloquia within the different phases of learning is crucial for maximizing their impact. Let's explore how these environments can be adapted for the Discovery Phase (ages 0-11) and the Scholar Phases.

Adapting Group Discussions and Colloquia for Learning Phases

Discovery Phase (Ages 0-11)

During the Discovery Phase, the focus is on building character, fostering curiosity, and developing a love for learning. Let's look at what this looks like once the child is around 6 years old through 11. Group discussions and colloquia at this stage should be tailored to support these goals:

- Use simple, guided discussions to reinforce moral lessons and character development.
- Implement "sharing circles" where children express thoughts on basic ethical concepts.
- Introduce storytelling sessions, followed by gentle questioning to encourage reflection.
- Create "wonder circles" where students share interesting facts they've discovered.
- Facilitate brief, topic-based discussions that encourage asking questions.

- Use guided explorations of age-appropriate subjects to spark curiosity and dialogue.

Scholar Phase

As students progress into the Scholar Phase, discussions and colloquia become more life-changing, aligning with their developing critical thinking skills:

Practice Scholar (12-14 years):
- Introduce structured Socratic discussions on foundational texts.
- Begin implementing formal colloquia with clear roles and expectations.
- Encourage students to lead portions of discussions under mentor guidance.

Apprentice Scholar (14-16 years):
- Deepen colloquia experiences with more complex texts and longer preparation times.
- Introduce cross-curricular discussions to help students make interdisciplinary connections.
- Assign rotating leadership roles in discussions to develop facilitation skills.

Self-Directed Scholar (14-18 years):
- Encourage students to organize and lead their own colloquia on chosen subjects.
- Implement advanced debate formats on complex historical or current event topics.
- Use discussions to explore real-world applications of learned principles.

Key Considerations Across Phases

1. **Gradual Complexity:** Increase the depth and complexity of discussions as students progress through the phases.

2. **Skill Development:** Focus on developing specific skills in each phase, from basic turn-taking to advanced argumentation.

3. **Mentor Role:** Adjust your role from primary facilitator in earlier phases to guide and occasional observer in later phases.

4. **Preparation:** Gradually increase expectations for pre-discussion preparation as students mature.

5. **Reflection:** Incorporate age-appropriate reflection activities after discussions to reinforce learning.

By thoughtfully adapting group discussions and colloquia to each learning phase, mentors can create engaging, developmentally appropriate experiences that foster critical thinking, communication skills, and collaborative learning throughout the educational journey.

The Structure of Effective Discussions

A successful group discussion begins with preparation. Participants are expected to come ready to engage, having studied the material beforehand. This pre-work involves more than just reading; it requires students to grapple with the ideas, challenge assumptions, make connections, and formulate thoughtful questions or comments.

The role of the mentor in these discussions is crucial but nuanced. Rather than lecturing, the mentor's primary task is to facilitate, guiding the conversation through thought-provoking questions. The mentor uses their spiritual eyes to find ways to relate the material to the students. The mentor also looks for what "forms" the classic is showing. For instance, if the material is "Romeo and Juliet,"[3] the following forms might be discussed:

- Feuds
- Forgiveness or the lack thereof
- Love and romance
- War
- Suicide

Whereas, if the material was Plato's "The Allegory of The Cave,"[4] the following forms and insights might be discussed:

- How does one find the truth?
- Slavery
- Growth
- How does one gain knowledge?
- What are forms of justice?
- Why is ignorance limiting? How do I find my ignorance?
- Pride

This approach encourages students to express their thoughts and feelings, leading to moments of self-awareness and personal breakthroughs.

Creating a Safe and Productive Environment

To ensure these discussions are productive, it's essential to create a safe environment where all participants feel comfortable sharing their ideas. This is achieved by establishing basic rules of respect, active listening, and open-minded opinion sharing. Remember, the goal is not to reach agreement on every point but to deepen understanding and refine ideas.

What Group Discussions Are Not

It's important to understand what these discussions should not become:

- **Lectures:** While the mentor may offer brief explanations, the focus should be on student engagement.
- **Personal storytelling sessions:** While personal experiences can illustrate points, they shouldn't dominate the discussion.
- **Problem-solving for personal issues:** The focus should remain on the material being discussed.
- **Platforms for personal agendas:** The discussion should serve the group's learning, not individual soap-boxing.

Colloquia: In-Depth Exploration

Colloquia offers a more structured and formal approach to collaborative learning designed to facilitate deep analysis and philosophical exploration. To expand on this important aspect of Leadership Education, consider the following elements:

Preparation for a Colloquium

Thorough preparation is crucial for a successful colloquium:

1. **Text selection:** Choose classic texts or significant works

that offer depth and complexity suitable for extended discussion.

2. **Pre-reading assignments**: Provide participants with reading materials well in advance, along with possible guiding questions to focus their study.

3. **Participant roles:** Consider assigning specific roles to participants on occasion, such as discussion leader, devil's advocate, or summarizer, to encourage active engagement.

The Mentor's Role in Colloquia

In a colloquium, the mentor's role focuses on thoughtfully guiding students through the material by asking probing questions that encourage deeper analysis. Throughout the discussion, mentors help participants discover connections between different texts and ideas while gently challenging assumptions to promote critical thinking. They maintain a high level of intellectual rigor while crafting questions that help students make personal connections with the material. Throughout this process, mentors actively seek to understand what forms—ways of doing and being—the material might be discussing, helping students uncover deeper meanings and applications.

Fostering Interdisciplinary Connections

One of the unique aspects of colloquia is their potential for interdisciplinary exploration. Mentors actively encourage participants to draw meaningful connections between the text and other disciplines, helping them discover how ideas transcend traditional subject boundaries. They guide students in exploring how the discussed ideas relate to contemporary issues and personal experiences, making ancient wisdom relevant to modern life. Through this approach, the text becomes a springboard for discussing broader philosophical and ethical questions, enriching understanding through multiple perspectives.

Techniques for Engaging Diverse Learners

Effective mentors employ various techniques to engage different types of learners:

1. **Writing before sharing**: After posing a question, allow students a few minutes to jot down their thoughts before discussing.

2. **Partner discussions:** In larger groups, have participants pair up to share their ideas before opening the floor to the whole group.

3. **Follow-up questions**: Use students' initial responses as springboards for deeper, more probing questions.

These methods ensure that all students have the opportunity to engage with the material and express their thoughts, regardless of their learning style or comfort level with public speaking.

The Importance of Time Management and Focus

Setting clear start and end times for discussions shows respect for participants' time and helps maintain focus. It's also crucial to keep the conversation on track, gently but firmly steering it back to the main topic if it veers too far off course.

The Ultimate Goal

Remember, the overarching aim of these discussions is to teach students *how* to think, not *what* to think. This means we want the students to be able to identify the forms – ways of doing and being – that the material is showing. The author is making a statement about those forms and the results of living by those forms. We want our students to use their own life experiences and other material they have read to discuss whether or not they agree or disagree with the author, and then to make more meaningful connections that inspire personal growth.

Let's continue by using the example of Plato's cave allegory.[5] One thing Plato is doing is showing the results of ignorance. The people in the cave who are chained to the wall and can turn their heads neither right nor left have only one point of reference by which to judge life. They can see the shadows across the way on the other side of the cave. They do not have an understanding of multiple sources of light or three-dimensional objects, only shadows. They don't have the language or experience to know what is actually real. Plato shows what he thinks ignorance is and what the lack of knowledge and light leads to. This can lead to a rich discussion about ignorance, what it is, and what we can do about it. Students can decide if they agree with Plato once they understand his line of logic and his platform. Once they can analyze his assumptions and line of reasoning, they can go to the next level and discuss if they agree or disagree. Then, they can look at the world around them and see if Plato's theory is relevant to their lives and what they are experiencing in the world, as well as what it means to them going forward.

By engaging in thoughtful, collaborative exploration of ideas, students learn to analyze, synthesize, and articulate their thoughts more effectively. They also benefit from the insights and perspectives of their peers, broadening their understanding and making connections.

In essence, well-conducted group discussions are powerful tools. They transform passive recipients of information into active, engaged thinkers capable of wrestling with complex ideas and articulating their own well-reasoned perspectives. Through this process, students not only deepen their understanding of the material at hand but also develop crucial skills for leadership and lifelong learning.

While discussions provide a foundation for collaborative learning, they represent just one facet of effective education. In the next chapter, we'll turn our attention to reading. We'll explore how the solitary pursuit of knowledge through text complements and enhances the interactive nature of group discussion, creating a richer tapestry of learning experiences that develop both independent thought and collaborative wisdom.

Let's Take a Deeper Look — Chapter 7

These questions aren't just for pondering – they're invitations to connect these ideas with your own journey and vision as an educator. Take time to explore them deeply, perhaps journaling your thoughts or discussing them with fellow mentors.

1. Consider your past experiences with group discussions or colloquia. How do they compare to the approach described in this chapter? What elements do you think were most effective in fostering deep understanding and critical thinking?

2. Reflect on the role of preparation in effective group discussions. How might your approach to reading and studying change if you knew you'd be participating in a colloquium on the material? How could this impact your overall learning?

3. Think about the balance between structure and freedom in group discussions. How can a mentor effectively guide the conversation without turning it into a lecture? Can you recall an instance where you've seen this done well?

4. Consider the various techniques for engaging diverse learners (writing before sharing, partner discussions, follow-up questions). Which of these do you think would be most effective for you personally? How might you implement these in a group setting you lead?

Group Discussion/Colloquia: The Art of Collaborative Learning

5. Reflect on the statement that the goal of these discussions is to teach "how to think, not what to think." How does this approach differ from traditional educational methods you've experienced? What potential benefits and challenges do you see in students learning to discuss various forms (the way of doing or being)?

6. Think about the importance of creating a safe environment for discussions. What specific actions can mentors and participants take to ensure everyone feels comfortable sharing their ideas? Have you been part of a group where this was done particularly well?

Resources for Deeper Learning:

The Mentor's Handbook by Aneladee Milne. Available at LEMIHomeschool.com[6]

Crucial Conversations by Joseph Grenny et al.

CHAPTER 8

Reading:
The Gateway to Critical Thinking and Deep Understanding

Picture a young man sitting in a dimly lit corner of a Baltimore kitchen, tracing letters by candlelight. The year is 1828, and Frederick Douglass[1] is breaking the law simply by learning to read. With each word he masters, he risks severe punishment – slave owners understood well that literacy could light a spark that no chains could contain.

They were right. As Douglass would later write, learning to read was his "pathway from slavery to freedom." But reading didn't just give him access to information – it transformed how he thought and understood the world. Late at night, poring over newspapers and political writings, he did more than absorb words; he wrestled with ideas, analyzed arguments, and began to see the deeper patterns that held slavery's injustice in place[2]. Each text he encountered became another step in his journey from understanding letters on a page to understanding – and ultimately fighting against – the complex systems of his time.

Through reading, Douglass developed something powerful: the ability to think critically about his world and articulate that understanding to others. He progressed from basic literacy to becoming one of history's most compelling voices for freedom, using the written word to craft arguments that would help change the course of American history. His journey from enslaved person to renowned leader and abolitionist shows us the true power of reading – not just as a skill, but as a gateway to deeper understanding and meaningful action in the world.

When parents and mentors truly grasp this transformative power of reading, it changes how we approach teaching it to our children. We begin to see that reading isn't just about moving through reading levels or completing books. It's about nurturing the kind of deep engagement with ideas that can transform minds and hearts.

In this chapter, we'll explore how to guide our students through this profound journey. We'll look at how reading develops, from those first tentative steps of sounding out words, to the careful analysis that marks a true scholar. We'll discuss practical strategies for engaging with different types of texts, and discover how mentors can support students in developing the kind of deep, critical reading skills that can help them understand and influence their world.

Through this exploration, we'll see how reading, when approached with purpose and depth, becomes more than just a basic skill; it becomes a powerful tool for developing leaders who can think critically, understand deeply, and act meaningfully in their communities and beyond.

Discovery Phase Reading (Ages 0-11)

During the Discovery Phase, children need to master the fundamental skills of reading and writing. There are many excellent methods for teaching these basics – from phonics programs to whole language approaches; structured literacy to natural learning methods. Parents should feel empowered to explore different approaches and use what works best for their individual child. Some children learn to read easily with minimal formal instruction, while others benefit from structured, systematic teaching. The key is recognizing and responding to each child's unique needs and learning style. By the time students reach Scholar Phase, they should be competent readers and writers, ready to engage with more complex texts and ideas. This foundation enables them to focus on deeper analysis and understanding rather than struggling with basic decoding and comprehension.

Reading daily to children from birth is one of the most powerful gifts we can give them. This consistent practice creates not only intellectual growth but deep emotional connections and family bonds.

Consider how reading together can transform relationships. When Tiffany's fifteen-year-old daughter Melanie was going through a rebellious stage, conflict with her ten-year-old brother Michael had created discord in their home. After using her spiritual eyes and pondering how to meet her children's needs, Tiffany began reading to them daily after lunch. She chose Owen Wister's classic *The Virginian*[3]. At first, the siblings sat on opposite sides of the room – if Michael got too close, Melanie would shoo him away. But within three weeks, something remarkable happened. Tiffany looked up one afternoon to find Melanie in the rocking chair with Michael beside her, her arm around him as they listened intently to the story. They followed this with *And There Was Light*[4], Jacques Lusseyran's inspiring biography about going blind at age eight and later leading France's underground newspaper during WWII. These shared reading experiences opened doors for meaningful conversations and rebuilt relationships between mother and daughter, brother and sister.

Daily reading benefits children in multiple ways. It develops their ability to visualize and imagine while building emotional intelligence through experiencing different perspectives in a safe environment. Through stories, children explore diverse ideas, cultures, and ways of being. They develop deeper awareness of themselves and others while building close family bonds and a natural love of learning.

This reading practice can adapt to any family's schedule – bedtime stories, morning reading sessions, or afternoon reading breaks. Siblings can read to each other, and audio books can supplement parent reading. As children grow, their engagement with books often deepens in unexpected ways. One mentor's precocious ten-year-old son demonstrated this after they finished *The Hobbit*[5] together.

When they began *The Lord of the Rings*[6], their reading sessions were so energetic that the mother lost her voice. Though he hadn't yet read such challenging books independently, the boy's desire to continue the story led him to finish the book by himself that month.

The Discovery Phase years offer a unique opportunity to establish reading as a joyful, connecting, family activity. When Tiffany expressed her desire to become a writer at age 18, her mentor advised her to "read a thousand books first." This wisdom applies equally to children – exposure to many voices and stories opens countless doors for future growth and understanding.

In these foundational years, we encourage parents and teachers to make reading together a consistent, cherished part of the daily routine. Through this practice, we nurture not just literacy but a lifelong love of learning and family connection.

Selecting Transformative Literature: The Power of Classics and Biographies

The choice of reading material profoundly impacts a student's development as both a scholar and a leader. Classics and biographies offer unique advantages in developing critical thinking and character.

Classics have earned their place in the canon by consistently engaging readers across time and cultures with fundamental human questions and experiences. When students read

Homer's *Odyssey*[7], they aren't just encountering an ancient adventure story—they're wrestling with timeless themes of loyalty, courage, and the meaning of home. These works have depth that rewards multiple readings.

Biographies serve a special role in Leadership Education by:

- Providing models of leadership and character through real-life examples.
- Demonstrating how individuals navigate challenges and moral dilemmas.
- Showing the development of leadership qualities over time.
- Connecting personal stories to larger historical movements.
- Inspiring students with examples of human potential.
- Making history real.

For example, reading about Thomas Edison's journey[8] from a struggling student to a renowned inventor can help students understand how challenges can become stepping stones to greatness.

Understanding Story Types: A Framework for Selection

Drawing from Daniel Taylor's *The Healing Power of Stories*[9], we can categorize books into four types that serve different purposes in a student's development:

1. **Whole Stories** These narratives present an intact world where good and evil are clearly defined, and justice prevails. They help establish a moral foundation and build confidence in younger readers. Examples include many folk tales and classic children's literature like *The*

Chronicles of Narnia [10].

2. **Broken Stories** These works honestly portray the brokenness in our world without offering resolution. While these stories have their place, especially in mature scholarly discussion, they should be balanced with other types to avoid fostering cynicism. Examples might include certain modern literary works that explore human suffering without redemption.

3. **Bent Stories** These narratives distort reality by presenting wrong as right or suggesting that truth is entirely relative. While older students might study these works to understand different worldviews, they require careful mentoring and strong foundational reading to engage with productively.

4. **Healing Stories** These works acknowledge brokenness but offer hope and the possibility of redemption. They help readers process difficult experiences and envision positive change. Examples include works like Viktor Frankl's *Man's Search for Meaning*[11] or Harper Lee's *To Kill a Mockingbird* [12].

Guidelines for Selection

When choosing books for students, consider:

- Developmental appropriateness
- What forms, ways of doing and being, the book is showing (more about forms later in the chapter).
- The balance of story types in their reading diet
- The student's current emotional and intellectual needs
- Opportunities for connection with other texts
- The potential for developing critical thinking skills

Types of Books

	Definition	Best Used For:	Phases:
Whole Stories	**Definition:** Stories presenting an intact world where good and evil are clearly defined and justice prevails.	**Best Used For:** • Build moral foundations • Early reading experiences • Establish trust in justice • Develop confidence	**Phases:** • Focus for Discovery • Continue for Practice and Apprentice Scholar • Balance for Self-Directed Scholar
Broken Stories	**Definition:** Stories that honestly portray the world's brokenness without offering clear resolution.	**Best Used For:** • Mature readers • Developing empathy • Understanding complexity • Critical thinking development	**Phases:** • Carefully introduce to Practice Scholars • Thoughtfully incorporate for Apprentice Scholar • Balance for Self-Directed Scholar
Bent Stories	**Definition:** Stories that distort reality by presenting wrong as right or suggesting truth is entirely relative	**Best Used For:** • Advanced scholars • Worldview analysis • Developing discrimination • Understanding propaganda	**Phases:** • Avoid for Discovery and Practice Scholar • Begin analyzing with guidance for Apprentice Scholar • Balance for Self-Directed Scholar
Healing Stories	**Definition:** Stories that acknowledge brokenness while offering hope and possibility of redemption.	**Best Used For:** • Processing difficult experiences • Building resilience • Understanding redemption • Personal growth	**Phases:** • Introduce for Discovery • Increase exposure for Practice & Apprentice Scholar • Balance for Self-Directed Scholar

Remember: The goal is not to avoid difficult content entirely but to introduce it thoughtfully and at developmentally appropriate times, always with adequate support and discussion.

(Taylor, 1996)

For example, in LEMI's Key of Liberty project (a Practice Scholar project), students read *Red Scarf Girl*[13] as a healing story that acknowledges the trauma of the Cultural Revolution while showing the resilience of the human spirit. This preparation helps them later engage with more complex works like *Wild Swans*[14] in QUEST (an Apprentice Scholar project), where they can analyze multiple perspectives on similar historical events.

Mentors should thoughtfully select different types of stories

The Learning Zone: Connecting Your Student's Heart, Mind & Purpose

throughout a student's development. They begin by introducing whole stories during the Discovery Phase to build strong moral foundations, then gradually incorporate healing stories as students develop greater emotional maturity. Broken stories are reserved for the Scholar Phase, when students have developed strong analytical skills to process more challenging narratives. Throughout this progression, mentors use bent stories sparingly and with careful guidance, helping students develop discernment in navigating complex moral and philosophical terrain.

By thoughtfully selecting reading material that aligns with these principles, mentors can create a rich literary environment that supports both intellectual growth and character development. This careful curation helps students progress naturally through the reading levels while developing the wisdom and discernment essential for leadership.

Understanding *what* we read lays the foundation for *how* we read. Just as a carpenter selects different tools for different tasks, readers need various approaches for engaging with different types of literature. The progression from whole stories to healing stories mirrors our development as readers, from basic comprehension to deeper analysis. A student reading *The Chronicles of Narnia*[15] as a whole story in their early years develops different skills than when they later encounter it as a healing story, discovering layers of meaning about faith, courage, and redemption. This deepening engagement with texts occurs through four distinct levels of reading, each building upon the previous one to develop increased comprehension and analytical abilities.

Reading Development Timeline

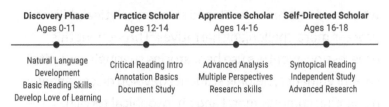

Discovery Phase	Practice Scholar	Apprentice Scholar	Self-Directed Scholar
Ages 0-11	Ages 12-14	Ages 14-16	Ages 16-18
Natural Language Development	Critical Reading Intro	Advanced Analysis	Syntopical Reading
Basic Reading Skills	Annotation Basics	Multiple Perspectives	Independent Study
Develop Love of Learning	Document Study	Research skills	Advanced Research

NOTE: Ages are approximate guidelines. Individual progression varies based on readiness.

Understanding the Four Levels of Reading

Drawing from Mortimer Adler and Charles Van Doren's seminal work *How to Read a Book*[16], developing a deep understanding of texts requires progressing through four distinct levels of reading. Each level builds on the previous one, leading students from basic word recognition to active, scholarly engagement with ideas across multiple works.

Level 1: Elementary Reading (Decoding)[17] This basic level involves recognizing and understanding individual words and simple sentences. It's the foundation upon which all other reading skills are built. We recognize this as a crucial starting point, but we don't stop here.

Children in the Discovery Level (ages 0-11) learn best through natural discovery and hands-on experiences. Here's how Elementary Reading might look at this stage:

Consider six-year-old Emma discovering the word "butterfly" while exploring her family's garden. Her mother doesn't rush to formally teach the word. Instead, she follows Emma's natural curiosity:

First, Emma points to a butterfly and says the word as she's heard it. Her mother then shows her the word in a nature book they're reading together. Emma notices that "butter" looks like a word she already knows from helping in the kitchen, and "fly" reminds her of watching insects in the garden. She begins to connect these familiar parts to decode the new word.

Later, Emma spots the word "butterfly" in other books and gets excited about recognizing it. This natural, discovery-based approach to decoding aligns perfectly with the Discovery Phase's emphasis on learning through real-life experiences and following the child's innate curiosity.

The mentor's role here is to create opportunities for organic discovery and celebration of these reading moments. This approach honors both the child's developmental stage and the principles of Leadership Education, where learning emerges naturally from meaningful experiences rather than forced instruction.

Level 2: Inspectional Reading (Basic Comprehension) [18]At this level, readers can grasp the main ideas of a text and summarize what they've read. While this is a step up from mere decoding, it still falls short of the deep engagement we aim for.

Consider 9-year-old Marcus encountering *The Tale of Despereaux*[19] for the first time. Rather than diving straight into detailed reading, he employs basic comprehension strategies that match his developmental stage:

First, Marcus explores the book's physical features. He examines the cover illustration of the brave mouse, flipping through the chapters, and noting the different character illustrations. His mentor, following the principles of the Discovery Phase, doesn't push for deep analysis but encourages this natural exploration by asking open-ended questions like "What do you notice about this book?" and "What do you think this story might be about?"

When Marcus begins reading, he focuses on grasping the main story line: a small mouse with big dreams who falls in love with a princess. He might summarize chapters in simple terms: "Despereaux isn't like other mice because he loves music and stories instead of crumbs." While he might miss some of the book's deeper themes about courage and forgiveness, he can follow the basic plot and describe key characters.

His mentor supports this level of reading by:

- Creating comfortable reading spaces that invite exploration.
- Allowing Marcus to share his discoveries without pressure for deeper analysis.
- Celebrating his ability to retell the story in his own words.
- Connecting the reading to his interests and experiences.

This approach honors the Discovery Phase described earlier, where students naturally progress from simple understanding to more complex engagement with material. It bridges basic decoding and the analytical reading that will come later in the Scholar Phase.

The focus remains on building confidence and enjoyment in reading, laying the foundation for deeper comprehension skills that will develop naturally as Marcus progresses.

Level 3: Analytical Reading (Critical Engagement)[20] This is where the Scholar Phase begins to take shape. Analytical reading is an active, intense process that involves:

- Asking probing questions about the text.
- Identifying the author's main arguments and supporting evidence.
- Evaluating the logic and validity of these arguments.
- Connecting the ideas to existing knowledge and other texts.

As Adler puts it, analytical reading is an exercise of the mind that moves the reader "from understanding less to understanding more."[21] This aligns perfectly with our goal of developing critical thinkers who can engage deeply with complex ideas.

Level 4: Syntopical Reading (Comparative Analysis) [22]This highest level of reading involves comparing and contrasting ideas across multiple texts. It's a complex, demanding process that requires:

- Reading multiple books on a single topic.
- Identifying relevant themes and ideas across these texts.
- Analyzing how different authors approach similar concepts.
- Synthesizing this information to form new insights.

Syntopical reading is where students truly become scholars. It's not just about understanding individual texts but about engaging in the "Great Conversation"[23] of ideas across time and disciplines. This reading level transforms students from passive recipients of information into active participants in creating knowledge and discussing forms.

Commonplace Books: A Scholar's Reading Companion

While annotation captures our immediate engagement with texts, Commonplace Books[24] provide a structured way to collect and organize the insights we gather through reading over time. Dating back centuries, these personal repositories have helped scholars from Leonardo da Vinci to Virginia Woolf develop their thinking and preserve valuable ideas.

A Commonplace Book differs from a simple journal or diary – it's a curated collection of quotes, ideas, and reflections organized for future reference and deeper understanding. For Leadership Education students, particularly in the Scholar Phase, maintaining a Commonplace Book can:

- Develop systematic thinking by organizing ideas across different texts and subjects.
- Deepen engagement with reading through purposeful

collection of meaningful passages.

- Create connections between seemingly unrelated concepts.
- Build a personal reference library of powerful ideas and insights.
- Support the transition from passive reading to active scholarship.

Students can begin with simple collections of favorite quotes and gradually develop more detailed systems for organizing and connecting ideas. The practice naturally supports progression through the reading levels – from basic collection of interesting passages to analytical comparison of ideas across texts.

Implementation Guidelines:

- Start with a dedicated notebook or digital document.
- Create clear categories for different types of entries.
- Include complete citations for future reference.
- Add personal reflections to connect ideas to experience.
- Review and revisit entries regularly to discover new connections.
- Share insights with peers during discussions and colloquia.

Through consistent use of a Commonplace Book, students develop not just reading comprehension but the habits of mind essential for scholarly thinking and leadership.

Introduction to Forms

In Leadership Education, forms are ways of doing and being – specific patterns of action, behavior, or thought that consistently lead to particular results. Just as certain mathematical formulas reliably produce specific outcomes, human behaviors and choices create predictable patterns of consequences.

Government systems provide clear examples of how different forms lead to predictable outcomes. When students study systems of government, they discover distinct patterns – what we call forms – of organizing and exercising power. Consider three fundamental forms: monarchy (rule by a king), tyranny (rule by force), and democratic republic (rule by elected representatives). Each form creates its own predictable patterns of relationship between rulers and citizens. Tyranny consistently produces oppression and loss of liberty, as seen throughout history from ancient Rome to modern dictatorships. Monarchies yield varying results based on the individual ruler's character and wisdom, as demonstrated by the contrast between enlightened monarchs like Marcus Aurelius and destructive ones like King John of England. Democratic republics, designed with inherent checks and balances, tend to better protect individual rights and promote citizen participation, though they face their own unique challenges and potential weaknesses.

Literature, particularly Shakespeare's plays, offers rich examples for studying forms – patterns of human behavior and their consequences. In *The Merchant of Venice*[25], Shakespeare examines two competing forms: unforgiving vengeance versus merciful justice. Through Shylock, we see how a lifetime of mistreatment created a pattern of bitterness that ultimately leads to seeking revenge through legal manipulation. This form – choosing vengeance over mercy – threatens to destroy both the target of revenge and the seeker. In contrast, Portia champions a different form through her famous speech about mercy:

> "The quality of mercy is not strain'd. It droppeth as the gentle rain from heaven Upon the place beneath. It is twice blest: It blesseth him that gives and him that takes.[26]"

This speech illuminates how mercy, as a form or way of living, creates a different pattern of results, blessing both the giver and receiver.

In *Romeo and Juliet*[27], Shakespeare examines the destructive form of generational feuding. The pattern is unmistakable: the Montagues and Capulets perpetuate a cycle of pride, unforgiveness, and retribution that passes from parent to child. This form produces predictable results – street brawls, duels, and deaths – yet the families persist in their hatred until it claims their most precious treasures: their children. Through their tragedy, Shakespeare illustrates a universal truth about the form of feuding: it creates an ever-widening circle of destruction that continues until someone has the courage to break the cycle.

A central aim of Leadership Education is developing students' ability to recognize and analyze forms in both literature and life. By learning to discern the patterns of behavior, choice, and consequence playing out around them, students develop critical thinking skills. They learn to ask: What forms are being lived out in this situation? What results do these forms consistently produce? What alternative forms might lead to better outcomes?

Learning to think on this level eventually leads to the students being able to live very meaningful lives by identifying forms, ways of being and living that they are passionate about, and promoting them.

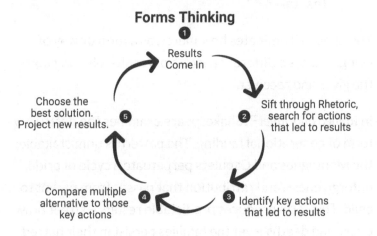

Forms Thinking

This kind of analysis doesn't develop overnight. It requires years of careful training through exposure to classics – works that have endured precisely because they offer profound insights into human forms and their consequences. Through guided study of these works, students gradually develop the ability to:

- Identify underlying patterns of behavior and thought.

- Analyze the relationship between choices and consequences.
- Compare different forms and their results across time and cultures.
- Apply these insights to contemporary challenges.

They then eventually learn to do the first half of solving a problem, that is to name the problem. If a desired result is lacking, a leader looks at the underlying form. If an awful outcome is happening, a leader looks at the underlying form. A leader looks at the underlying forms to find problems and solutions. Once a problem is named and defined accurately, then solutions (alternate forms, processes, and ways of doing something) can be created and pursued. This process goes hand in hand with cultivating character and a love for their fellow human beings.

The Progression of Forms Analysis Through Reading Levels

As students advance through the four reading levels, their ability to recognize and analyze forms naturally deepens. Let's examine how this development occurs:

Elementary Reading (Level 1)

At this foundational level, students begin to recognize basic patterns within individual texts. They identify simple cause-and-effect relationships while recognizing that certain behaviors lead to predictable outcomes. For example, a student reading Aesop's fables[28] might notice how pride consistently leads to downfall, or how wisdom consistently brings better results than foolishness.[29]

Inspectional Reading (Level 2)

As reading comprehension grows, students start recognizing similar patterns across different stories and seeing how authors use forms to convey messages. A student at this level reading *The Merchant of Venice*[30] might recognize the basic conflict between mercy and vengeance, though they may not yet grasp all its implications.[31]

Analytical Reading (Level 3)

Here students develop deeper understanding of forms through careful analysis. They examine how authors intentionally use forms to reveal truth while understanding complex relationships between different forms. At this level, students studying *Romeo and Juliet*[32] can analyze how the form of feuding creates ripple effects throughout the entire play, understanding both immediate and long-term consequences of this destructive pattern.[33]

Syntopical Reading (Level 4)

This highest level enables a meaningful forms analysis as students compare how different authors treat similar forms and connect historical patterns to contemporary situations. For instance, a student might compare the treatment of tyranny across multiple works – from historical accounts of ancient Rome to Shakespeare's political plays, the *Federalist Papers*[34], and modern political analysis.[35]

This progression allows students to move from simple pattern recognition to advanced analysis of forms in both literature and life. Through careful study at each level, they develop increasingly nuanced understanding of human nature and deeper insight into the consequences of choices.

The ultimate goal is developing leaders who can identify underlying forms in complex situations and help others understand and navigate forms effectively. This progression requires patience and careful mentoring, with each level building upon previous understanding to create an increasingly refined ability to recognize and analyze forms across all types of reading and real-world situations.

Developing Advanced Reading Skills

As students progress from basic comprehension toward syntopical reading, they need to develop both broad reading strategies and specific analytical skills. Document Studies and annotation serve as two powerful tools for developing these advanced capabilities.

Document Studies: A Foundation for Advanced Reading

Document Studies represent a distinct and powerful learning environment in their own right, worthy of detailed exploration beyond the scope of this chapter. These focused examinations of primary sources and significant texts provide an ideal framework for developing critical reading and analytical skills. Through Document Studies, students learn to:

- Analyze primary sources systematically.
- Take the time to look up definitions, historical context, and reach deeper for understanding.

- Engage deeply with challenging texts.
- Develop historical and contextual understanding.
- Build critical thinking capabilities.
- Identify the author's base assumptions, line of logic, and conclusions.
- Connect ideas across different documents.

The Role of Annotation in Advanced Reading

Document Studies offers an excellent opportunity to teach annotation, a skill that then transfers to all types of reading. Through annotation, students create visible evidence of their thinking process, much like a scientist recording observations in a lab notebook. This systematic approach transforms reading from a passive activity into an active, documented journey of discovery.

Key Components of Annotation:
- A deep, thorough reading
- Identify and follow the author's reasoning using marginal notes
- Recognize patterns and themes through systematic highlighting
- Look up meanings and cross-reference ideas and topics
- Connect ideas using visual aids, like arrows and brackets
- Create a personal dialogue with the text through questioning marks and comments
- Thoughtful analysis of which forms are being discussed

The Document Study Process with Integrated Annotation:

1. Pre-reading

- Study historical context to set up the framework.
- Preview text features and mark areas for focused attention.
- Note initial questions and predictions in margins.
- Create a personal system of symbols for the document.
- Record background knowledge and context.

Whether working with shorter documents or full-length books, previewing text features helps students identify areas of focus and prepare for active engagement. By annotating chapter headings or introductory sections in books, students can create a roadmap for deeper reading and mark initial questions or key themes.

2. Close Reading

- Highlight key ideas and forms (using restraint to maintain emphasis).
- Write marginal notes summarizing the main points.
- Mark areas of confusion with specific questions.
- Draw connections between sections using visual cues.

Close reading, whether applied to a brief document or a chapter of a book, benefits from strategic annotation. Highlighting key ideas and summarizing main points in the margins allows students to maintain a continuous dialogue with the text. This approach helps them track significant moments and note their reflections throughout the reading journey, ensuring comprehension in both shorter and longer texts.

3. Questioning

- Mark different types of questions with distinct symbols, like the following:
  ○ "?" for basic comprehension questions.
  ○ "?!" for surprising or contradictory information.
  ○ "★?" for deeper analytical questions.
- Note possible answers in the margins as they emerge.
- Track patterns of questions to identify areas needing clarification.
- Create a dialogue with the text through margin comments and responses.

4. Analysis

- Underline key evidence and arguments.
- Use margin notes to evaluate logic and validity.
- Create shorthand symbols for recurring themes or ideas.
- Mark connections to other sources with specific citations.
- Note historical context and perspective in brackets.
- Watch which forms are being discussed.

5. Making Connections

- Draw arrows between related ideas within the text and even beyond the text.
- Be still and ponder, letting ideas come to mind.
- Use margin numbers or letters to link connected passages.

- Create summary boxes connecting multiple concepts.
- Note references to other texts or outside knowledge.
- Develop personal symbols for tracking broader themes.

6. Discussion Preparation

- Star or highlight key points about the forms and ideas for group discussion.
- Summarize the main arguments at the end of the section.
- Note potential discussion questions.
- Mark passages that need clarification from peers.
- Record initial responses to share.

Mentor Tips for Supporting Annotation:

Mentors support annotation skill development in multiple ways: sharing their own annotated texts as examples, creating targeted annotation guides for different types of documents, and regularly reviewing student annotations to gauge understanding. They use these annotated texts as the foundation for individual conferences while guiding students in developing personalized annotation systems that work best for their learning style. Remember that effective annotation, like any skill, develops over time. As students progress through increasingly complex texts, their annotation systems should evolve to meet new challenges and deeper levels of analysis.

Extending Annotation to Book Reading

Annotating book-length texts requires different strategies than annotating shorter documents to maintain engagement and manage the larger scope effectively. Rather than marking every detail, students should focus on:

- Creating chapter summaries that track major developments and connect to broader themes. After completing each chapter, write a brief synthesis in the book's margin or in a separate notebook, highlighting how it builds on previous chapters.
- Tracking new vocabulary and ideas.
- Using a tiered annotation system: Mark major plot points, character developments, or argumentative turns with distinct symbols (★ for pivotal moments, △ for significant character changes), while using simpler marks for supporting details. This hierarchy helps maintain clarity when reviewing the text later.
- Building a progressive theme tracker: Rather than annotating every instance of a theme, mark significant evolution points. For example, if tracking the theme of justice in a novel, only mark moments where the concept of justice notably shifts or develops.
- Creating periodic way points: Every few chapters, pause to write a brief connecting note that links major ideas or developments from recent sections to earlier parts of the book. This helps maintain awareness of larger patterns without getting lost in details.
- Writing about the forms being shown in the book.

This focused approach helps students maintain consistent engagement with longer texts while avoiding annotation fatigue. Most importantly, it creates a useful map of the book's key ideas and developments that supports deeper analysis and discussion.

Guiding Students with Learning Challenges

In our pursuit of Leadership Education, it's crucial to recognize that every student's journey is unique, and some face additional challenges in their learning process. Learning differences like dyslexia can present significant obstacles, particularly in the realm of reading. However, with the right approach and support, these students can not only overcome these challenges but also develop unique strengths that contribute to their potential.

Consider one of Tiffany's sons who struggled significantly with reading. While some children seemed to pick up reading effortlessly, Tiffany spent hundreds of hours working with her son to help him learn to read. This experience illustrates how different children have different learning paces and strengths. Interestingly, the same son who struggled with reading was able to ride a bike without training wheels at just three years old, demonstrating exceptional physical coordination and balance.

This story highlights a crucial principle: each child has unique strengths and challenges. While Tiffany's son faced difficulties with reading, he excelled in other areas. As mentors, our role is to recognize and nurture these individual differences, providing support where needed while also celebrating and developing each student's unique talents. Tiffany's son became an avid reader using audio

Reading: The Gateway to Critical Thinking & Deep Understanding reading. He often reads/listens to a book a day, as he learned to listen between 3 and 8 times the speed on most devices. His note-taking took on an unusual dimension as well. By using other technology, where he dictated his notes into his device from memory rather than seeing and reading the text, he developed exceptional memory skills.

Insights into Dyslexia and Other Learning Differences

Dyslexia is a specific learning difference that primarily affects reading and related language-based processing skills. It's important to understand that it is not related to intelligence. It affects individuals differently, and to varying degrees, and with appropriate support, individuals with dyslexia can achieve high levels of academic and professional success.

Other learning challenges might include dysgraphia (difficulty with writing), dyscalculia (difficulty with math), or ADHD (attention deficit hyperactivity disorder). Each of these present unique challenges and require tailored support.

Example of Thomas Edison's Strengths Despite Learning Challenges:

Thomas Edison's[36] early school years were marked by significant academic struggles. His teacher considered him "addled," and he lasted only three months in formal schooling before his mother began teaching him at home. However, Edison found his strengths through hands-on experimentation and self-directed learning. Despite his challenges with traditional education, he developed into an avid reader and learner, devouring books on subjects that interested him and conducting countless experiments. His mother's belief in his potential and support of his unique learning style helped him develop into one of history's most prolific inventors. Edison's example reminds us that learning differences do not preclude greatness. When mentors support students in nurturing their unique strengths— whether they involve hands-on learning, problem-solving, or creative thinking—these students can excel and make profound contributions to society.

The Power of Embracing Neurodiversity

We recognize that diversity of thought and experience enriches our learning communities. Students with learning challenges like dyslexia bring unique perspectives and problem-solving approaches that can enhance group discussions and collaborative projects.

By providing appropriate support and leveraging their strengths, we can help these students not just overcome challenges but truly excel. In doing so, we prepare them for leadership roles where their unique cognitive profiles can be significant assets.

Remember, some of history's greatest leaders and innovators, from Leonardo Da Vinci to Richard Branson, have had dyslexia[37]. Our role as mentors is to nurture the potential in every student, recognizing that sometimes the greatest strengths can emerge from our greatest challenges.

Allowing, fostering, and facilitating alternate learning methods is a key factor in helping those with dyslexia. This doesn't mean the child never reads; it just means that the difficulty with reading won't slow down the assimilation of material or learning.

Harnessing Reading as a Transformative Tool

Reading is not just about acquiring information; it's about transforming hearts and minds and shaping future leaders. By developing advanced reading skills, students learn to think critically, engage with complex ideas, and participate in the ongoing dialogue of human knowledge.

As mentors, our role is to guide students through this journey, helping them progress from basic comprehension to the heights of syntopical reading. In doing so, we equip them with one of the most powerful tools for lifelong learning and leadership: the ability to engage deeply and critically with the written word.

Remember, in the words of Francis Bacon, "Reading maketh a full man; conference a ready man; and writing an exact man."[38] Through reading, we prepare our students not only to be full of knowledge, but to be ready to engage with the world and to articulate their own ideas with precision and power.

With reading as the gateway to understanding and growth, it naturally leads us to the next crucial step: writing. Writing transforms comprehension into expression, empowering students to crystallize their thoughts and share their perspectives. In the following chapter, we will explore the Writing Learning Environment—where students learn to hone their voices, express ideas with clarity, and participate actively in the ongoing dialogue of human thought.

Let's Take a Deeper Look — Chapter 8

These questions aren't just for pondering – they're invitations to connect these ideas with your own journey and vision as an educator. Take time to explore them deeply, perhaps journaling your thoughts or discussing them with fellow mentors.

1. Think about your current reading habits. Which of Adler's four levels of reading do you most often engage in? How might you incorporate more analytical and syntopical reading into your routine?

2. Reflect on a time when you successfully guided a student through a document study. What strategies were most effective? How can you incorporate these elements into future reading instruction?

3. Consider the annotation techniques described in the chapter. Which of these do you currently use, and which would you like to incorporate? How might you teach these techniques to your students?

4. The chapter emphasizes the importance of creating an effective reading environment. How does your current learning space support or hinder the development of advanced reading skills? What changes could you make to better foster active engagement, reflection, and collaborative learning around texts?

5. The chapter discusses strategies for supporting students with learning challenges. How can you adapt your teaching methods to better accommodate diverse learners while still promoting advanced reading skills?

Resources for Deeper Learning:

How to Read a Book: The Classic Guide to Intelligent Reading, by Mortimer J. Adler and Charles Van Doren[39]

Healing Power of Stories, by Daniel Taylor[40]

The Dyslexic Advantage: Unlocking the Hidden Potential of the Dyslexic Brain," by Brock L. Eide and Fernette F. Eide[41]

LEMIWorks! Podcast episodes "Transfer of Soul," "Why Do We Read?" and "Quality Mentoring," available at LEMIWorks.com[42]

Liber Connect by Tiffany Earl available at LEMIHomeschool.com

CHAPTER 9

Writing: Developing Voice and Vision

Julie spent hours crafting her essay about her grandmother's immigration journey. The words flowed naturally as she described her grandmother's courage in leaving everything behind, her struggles learning English, and the determination that led to opening a small restaurant. Julie felt proud sharing such a personal story, knowing she had captured the essence of her grandmother's spirit.

A week later, her essay returned covered in red ink. Every grammatical error, spelling mistake, and structural flaw was marked. Her teacher had even noted that some of her grandmother's quoted expressions weren't proper English. While the comments were technically accurate, they completely missed the heart of Julie's work. Her pride turned to shame, and the once-confident writer retreated into silence. It would be months before she willingly shared her writing again.

This experience, unfortunately common in traditional education, illustrates why we must fundamentally rethink our approach to writing. Writing is not merely a technical skill to be corrected and refined; it is one of the most potent tools for developing and expressing ideas, thoughts, feelings, and experiences. Writing serves as both a means of communication and a crucial learning environment—one where voice and meaning must precede mechanics, where self-expression leads naturally to skill development, and where the heart of the writer is nurtured alongside their craft.

Consider two contrasting approaches to writing development:

The first treats writing as primarily a technical skill. This approach focuses on structure, grammar, and form. While these elements matter, emphasizing them too early can silence a writer's emerging voice. Julie's experience demonstrates how well-intentioned correction can actually impede growth when it comes at the wrong time or in the wrong way.

The second approach, which we embrace in Leadership Education, views writing as a natural journey of discovery and expression. Like a gardener nurturing a seedling, this method provides the right support at the right time. Technical skills are still developed, but they grow naturally from a student's desire to express their ideas more effectively. When students have something meaningful to say—when they understand the power of their words to influence others and shape the world—they become motivated to master the tools of effective communication.

This chapter explores how mentors can guide students through this transformative journey, helping them develop both their unique voice and the skills to express it effectively. We'll examine:

- How writing serves as both expression and discovery.
- The natural progression of writing development.
- Specific strategies for mentoring different phases of growth.
- Ways to address common challenges while maintaining enthusiasm.
- Methods for balancing creative freedom with technical development.

Through understanding and implementing these principles, mentors can help students avoid Julie's experience and instead discover writing as a powerful tool for personal growth, intellectual development, and meaningful impact in the world.

The LEMI Writing Philosophy

Writing serves as both a means of expression and a pathway to discovery. Like a two-sided mirror, it allows us to project our thoughts outward while simultaneously reflecting them back for deeper examination. This dual nature makes writing an invaluable tool in developing future leaders who can both communicate effectively and think deeply.

Corrie Ten Boom tells of an experience when she spent months in solitary confinement during World War II[1]. The guards let a package get transferred to her they thought was innocuous and held no meaning other than saying Happy Birthday. Unbeknownst to them, she gently removed the stamp, and underneath it, discovered a message. The clocks had been delivered. In code, she was told that the children she and her family had been hiding, were safe. She broke down in tears. This written communication was small indeed, fitting underneath a stamp. It makes us wonder, why do we write? Why do we communicate? What's so important that we would learn a written language in order to disseminate it, and take such risks in time, resources, and efforts in doing so?

The answers to these questions are personal, and we ask our students to reach deep and to think about them.

Writing as Expression

When Heidi worked with a high school student who struggled to write even a single paragraph, everything changed when she discovered his passion for Parkour, an athletic training discipline. Once he began writing about something that mattered to him, the words flowed naturally. Within a week, he had written three pages and was actively seeking feedback to improve his work. This transformation illustrates a fundamental principle: authentic expression emerges naturally when students have something meaningful to say.

Writing as expression encompasses several key elements that work together to create meaningful communication. It involves the process of articulating thoughts and feelings clearly, while also sharing ideas and perspectives in ways that resonate with others. Through written expression, writers can influence others through their carefully chosen words, actively contribute to ongoing dialogues on important topics, and create meaningful connections between ideas and with their readers. This multifaceted approach to writing allows for both personal growth and engagement with broader conversations.

Writing as Discovery

As novelist E.M. Forster famously asked, "How do I know what I think until I see what I say?[2]" Writing serves as a powerful tool for exploring and clarifying our thoughts. Consider Emma, a Scholar Phase student who kept a commonplace book while studying the American Revolution. As she collected quotes and added her own reflections, she discovered connections between historical events and modern challenges. She didn't just record information through writing; she developed new insights and deeper understanding.

Writing serves as a powerful tool for discovery, enabling writers to explore and clarify their thoughts while testing and refining their ideas through the writing process. As writers engage with their material, they often make unexpected connections between concepts, leading to the development of new perspectives. Through this journey of written exploration, writers achieve a deeper understanding not just of their subject matter, but often of themselves and their relationship to the ideas they're exploring.

The Writing Cycle

Just as children learn to walk before they run, writing development follows a natural progression. The LEMI Writing Cycle provides a framework for understanding and supporting this journey:

1. **Listening:** The natural state of being and soaking in knowledge.

2. **Speaking:** The foundation of oral and written communication.

3. **Narration:** Retelling stories and experiences.

4. **Creation:** Developing original stories and ideas.

5. **Journaling/Storytelling:** Bridging oral and written expression.

6. **Opinion Writing:** Developing and expressing viewpoints.

7. **Persuasion:** Supporting views with evidence and logic.

8. **Research:** Synthesizing multiple sources and perspectives.

This progression isn't rigid but rather guides mentors in providing appropriate support at each stage. Consider Mattias, who began his writing journey by drawing pictures in a dream journal. His mother wisely recognized this as valid self-expression and supported his development by writing down his verbal explanations of the drawings. This approach honored his current stage while gently guiding him toward written expression.

Writing as a Bridge

Writing serves as a crucial bridge between abstract thought and concrete action. Once ideas are captured on paper, they become tangible entities that can be examined, refined, and developed. This process is particularly vital in Leadership Education, where we aim to develop individuals who can:

- Transform thoughts into clear expression
- Move from ideas to implementation
- Connect personal insights to broader impact
- Build understanding across perspectives
- Create meaningful change through words

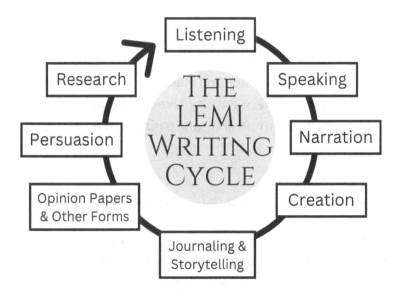

The power of writing as a bridge becomes evident when students begin to see how their words can influence others and shape the world around them. This vision of writing as a tool for impact often provides the motivation needed to master more technical aspects of the craft.

This philosophy informs every aspect of how we mentor writing, from how we structure assignments to how we provide feedback. By understanding writing as both expression and discovery, honoring natural development stages, and recognizing its role as a bridge to action, we can create environments where students develop not just as writers, but as thinkers and leaders.

Mentoring Writing Through The Phases

Discovery Phase (Ages 0-11): Nurturing Natural Expression

During the Discovery Phase, the focus is on developing a natural love for expression and building foundational writing skills through discovery and play. Like a young plant, writing abilities need gentle nurturing and patience to grow strong roots.

Core Principles:
- Let writing emerge naturally from listening to speaking and and then to storytelling.
- Honor individual developmental readiness.
- Support progression from drawing to writing.
- Allow dictation as a bridge to written expression.
- Celebrate all forms of communication.
- Listen and respond to early communication attempts from the child.

Ages 0-5

- Parents listen and respond to early communications, showing the child interest, love, and that attempts at communicating work.
- Not only do particular sound patterns mean specific things to a young baby, but most children are also capable of communicating through sign language if taught simple expressions. This gives young children relief and joy that simple needs are responded to like: more, water, please, all done, etc.
- When a child is listened to, it helps them develop a feeling of confidence and their worth is acknowledged .
- A young child is in a natural state of curiosity, a state of being where listening is just part of being. In this state they are gaining knowledge rapidly, including language.
- Introduce coloring, learning the alphabet, and writing, along with daily reading to them.

Ages 6-8

- Encourage drawing with storytelling.
- Welcome invented spelling.
- Scribe child-dictated stories.
- Use movement activities for writing muscles.
- Keep sessions brief and playful.
- Parent models writing though journaling and other means.
- Introduce your chosen method of learning to read and write.

Ages 9-11

- Introduce simple journaling.
- Write about personal experiences.

- Create basic stories and poems.
- Write letters and creative pieces.

Supporting students' writing growth requires a thoughtful, nurturing approach that begins with creating an environment conducive to creativity. This includes providing diverse writing materials and comfortable spaces where students can work. Mentors play a crucial role by modeling their own joy in writing and sharing their work, while maintaining focus on ideas and expression rather than getting caught up in mechanics too early. By keeping writing tasks short and engaging, and consistently celebrating effort and progress, mentors help maintain students' enthusiasm for writing.

Throughout this process, it's essential to remember several key principles. The joy of writing should remain central to the experience, with emphasis placed on the process of writing rather than just the final product. Since every child develops at their own unique pace, mentors must adjust their expectations and support accordingly. Building confidence takes precedence over correcting technical elements, particularly in the early stages. Finally, helping students connect their writing to real-life experiences makes the process more meaningful and engaging, fostering natural growth in their writing abilities.

This phase sets the stage for all future writing development. Success comes not through perfection but through nurturing a love for written expression while building basic skills through joyful exploration.

Practice Scholar Phase (Ages 12-14): Finding Voice and Building Confidence

During the Practice Scholar phase, the primary goal is to help students discover their unique voice and develop confidence in their ability to express themselves. Like a vocal coach who first helps singers find their natural range before teaching technique, mentors focus on encouraging authentic expression before emphasizing technical precision.

Creating a Safe Environment for Expression

- Respond first to ideas and content, not mechanics.
- Ask questions that deepen thinking rather than pointing out errors.
- Celebrate unique perspectives and creative approaches.
- Provide opportunities for low-stakes writing practice.
- Create regular sharing opportunities in supportive settings.
- When reading their papers ask, "What is my student saying, feeling, and thinking?"

For example, when Jamie submitted an emotionally raw piece about her parents' divorce, her mentor responded first to the courage it took to share such personal thoughts. Only after Jamie felt heard and validated did they begin discussing ways to strengthen the impact of her message.

Teaching the Six Points of Editing Without Crushing Creativity

While inspiring the desire for the student to learn great grammar and punctuation in personal writing so that they can get their messages across effectively, mentors can also start introducing editing principles through structured lessons. These will be further emphasized in the Apprentice Scholar phase as well, by asking the students to edit their own writing by figuratively wearing the following six different "editing hats."

1. Target Audience

   - Help students understand how tone changes for different readers.
   - Practice adapting writing style for various purposes.
   - Consider who would most benefit from or be most interested in the message.
   - Encourage writing for diverse audiences beyond peers and mentors.
   - Guide students in choosing vocabulary and tone appropriate for their chosen audience.

2. Content Relevance

   - Guide students in selecting and organizing ideas using Know, Feel, Do framework.
   - Help develop clear thesis statements that drive the content.
   - Teach discrimination between essential and peripheral information.
   - Encourage variety in types of evidence and proofs.
   - Support effective use of historical patterns, logic, reason, emotion, and quotes.

3. Structure and Form

   - Introduce basic organizational patterns.

- Practice logical flow of ideas.
- Guide decisions about thesis placement.
- Teach effective introduction techniques (hooks, road maps).
- Develop strong conclusion strategies.
- Balance creative expression with clear organization.

4. Flow

- Practice smooth transitions between ideas.
- Ensure logical progression of thoughts.
- Identify and fill gaps in reasoning.
- Create coherent connections between paragraphs.
- Maintain reader engagement through smooth progression.

5. Punctuation and Grammar

- Teach basic rules through separate exercises.
- Practice editing sample texts rather than personal writing.
- Reference reliable style guides (like Elements of Style).[3]
- Build credibility through proper mechanics.
- Remember this is important but shouldn't overshadow voice and content.

6. Readability

- Consider visual presentation and page layout.
- Ensure adequate white space and balance.
- Create clear paragraph breaks.
- Use appropriate formatting.
- Make the text inviting to read.

Implementation Guidelines:

- Introduce these points gradually.
- Focus on one or two aspects at a time.
- Use peer review to practice identifying these elements.
- Provide examples of both effective and ineffective writing.
- Celebrate progress in each area.
- Remember that content and voice should always take precedence over perfect mechanics.

Through careful attention to these six points, students develop their editing skills while maintaining their authentic voice and creativity. The goal is to help them become more effective communicators without dampening their enthusiasm for writing.

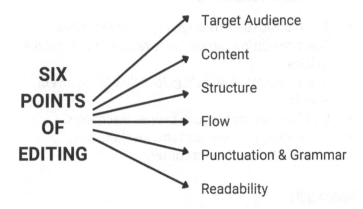

Apprentice Scholar Phase (Ages 14-16): Developing Deeper Understanding

As students progress to the Apprentice Scholar phase, they're ready to focus more on their craft while maintaining their authentic voice. Like a master craftsman teaching an eager apprentice, mentors now introduce more tools and techniques, like the six points of editing. Building on this foundation, students learn to strengthen their arguments through C.S. Lewis' Four Proofs of Reasoning. These proofs were identified by Aneladee Milne and Tiffany Earl through their careful study of Lewis' work, revealing the systematic way he built compelling arguments through reason, personal experience, revelation, and historicity.[4]

Incorporating C.S. Lewis' Four Proofs of Reasoning

1. Reason

   - Teach logical argument construction.
   - Practice step-by-step reasoning.
   - Example: Building a case for later school start times:
     - Premise: Teenagers naturally stay up later
     - Evidence: Sleep research data
     - Conclusion: Later starts would improve performance

2. Personal Experience

   - Show how to balance personal stories with objective evidence.
   - Guide appropriate use of anecdotal support.
   - Example: Connecting personal music education benefits to broader research on cognitive development

3. Revelation

   - Discuss appropriate integration of faith-based

insights.
- Practice a respectful presentation of beliefs.
- Example: Combining religious teachings about honesty with sociological research on trust

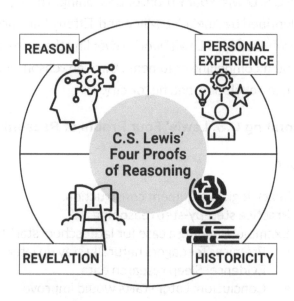

4. Historicity

- Teach effective use of historical evidence.
- Practice drawing parallels between past and present.
- Example: Analyzing how past communication changes (like telephone) inform understanding of social media impacts

Supporting Technical Growth

During this phase, mentors can support students' development through several key strategies. By gradually introducing more rigorous editing expectations, mentors help students build their technical skills without overwhelming them. They teach specific techniques for different writing forms while providing detailed feedback on both content and structure. Through careful guidance, mentors help students develop their own editing process, ensuring they can eventually work independently. Throughout this process, mentors assist students in finding the delicate balance between creative expression and technical precision, ensuring neither element is sacrificed for the other.

The key is maintaining students' confidence while helping them develop better writing skills. As one mentor observed, "We're not asking them to silence their voice, but to make it more powerful through careful craft."

Common Elements Across Phases

Regardless of phase, effective mentoring includes:

- Regular writing opportunities
- Constructive, encouraging feedback
- Clear, achievable challenges
- Celebration of progress
- Connection to meaningful purposes
- Introducing classics like *The Elements of Style* for teaching grammar and punctuation.[5]

Remember: The goal isn't perfect papers but confident writers who can think deeply and communicate effectively. Through patient mentoring that respects developmental stages while maintaining high standards, students often surprise themselves—and their mentors—by achieving what once seemed impossible.

Progressive Writing Forms

Writing ability develops naturally from simple expression to complex argumentation. Like musicians advancing from basic scales to intricate compositions, students become better writers.

Journaling/Storytelling: Building Voice Through Personal Expression

Journaling and storytelling serve as foundational bridges between thought and written expression, providing safe spaces for students to develop their writing voice and basic narrative skills.

Key Elements
- Personal reflection and observations
- Chronological sequencing
- Descriptive language
- Authentic voice
- Natural flow
- Emotional expression

Example Development Process

Consider Emma, a student beginning to explore written expression through journaling about her family's move to a new home:

Initial Entry: "We moved today."

Guided Development:
1. Mentor asked: "What details could help readers see and

feel what happened?"

2. Emma expanded with sensory details:
   - What she saw (empty rooms, moving boxes)
   - What she heard (truck engine, goodbye calls)
   - How she felt (excited, nervous)

3. Mentor helped organize the narrative chronologically and possibly acted as scribe

4. Final entry expressed both events and emotions while maintaining her authentic voice

Skills Developed:
- Observation and detail recognition
- Sequential thinking
- Descriptive writing
- Emotional awareness
- Voice development
- Basic narrative structure

While personal journaling builds foundational writing skills, scholars can also benefit from maintaining a Commonplace Book (as discussed in Chapter 8) alongside their journal. Where journals capture personal reflections and experiences, Commonplace Books collect and organize meaningful quotes and ideas encountered through reading. Together, these practices create a rich dialogue between personal expression and scholarly engagement. Students often find that passages collected in their Commonplace Books naturally inspire their own writing, while journal entries help them process and personalize the ideas they've gathered through reading.

Through journaling and storytelling, students build the foundational skills needed for more complex writing forms while developing confidence in their ability to express themselves through written words. This creates a natural progression toward opinion writing and more advanced forms of expression.

Opinion Papers: Finding Voice and Structure

Opinion papers serve as an entry point into academic writing, allowing students to develop their voice while learning basic argumentative structure. These papers typically emerge naturally from students' passionate interests and strong views.

Key Elements

- Clear position statement
- Personal reasoning
- Basic supporting examples
- Authentic voice
- Natural organization

Example Development Process

Consider Marcus, a student passionate about skateboarding in public spaces. His writing journey proceeded as follows:

Initial Position: "Skateboarding should be allowed downtown."

Guided Development:

1. Mentor asked: "Why do you believe this?"

2. Marcus listed the reasons:

- Provides healthy activity for teens
- Builds community
- Cheaper than building skate parks

3. The mentor helped organize ideas into a coherent flow

4. The final paper expressed his viewpoint while maintaining his authentic voice

Skills Developed:
- Articulating beliefs clearly
- Supporting opinions with reasons
- Basic logical organization
- Confidence in expression

Persuasive Essays: Building Stronger Arguments

Persuasive essays build on opinion writing by introducing more rigorous argumentation and consideration of opposing viewpoints. This form challenges students to move beyond personal opinion to create compelling cases for their positions.

Key Elements
- Well-defined thesis
- Multiple supporting arguments
- Evidence incorporation
- Counter-argument address
- Logical structure

Example Development Process

Sarah's essay advocating for extended library hours demonstrates this progression:

Initial Approach:

- Stated opinion: "The library should stay open later."
- Listed personal reasons: "I need more study time."

Mentor Guidance:

1. Encouraged research into:
   - Current usage patterns
   - Student study habits
   - Similar libraries' hours

2. Helped identify stakeholder concerns:
   - Budget implications
   - Staffing needs
   - Security considerations

Final Product:

Balanced argument incorporating:

- Statistical evidence
- Expert opinions
- Cost-benefit analysis
- Solutions to potential problems

Skills Developed:

- Research integration
- Logical argumentation
- Stakeholder consideration
- Solution development

Research Papers: Academic Writing

Research papers represent the culmination of student writing development, combining personal insight with scholarly analysis. This form requires thinking and careful integration of multiple sources.

Key Elements
- Original thesis
- Extensive research
- Source synthesis
- Academic conventions
- Complex argumentation

Example Development Process

Emma's research paper on social media's impact on teenage mental health illustrates this approach:

Preparation Phase:

1. Initial Research
    - Academic studies
    - Professional articles
    - Expert interviews
    - Current statistics

2. Thesis Development
    - Started broad: "Social media affects teens"
    - Refined through research: "While social media can enhance connection, unstructured use significantly impacts teenage anxiety levels, suggesting the need for guided engagement strategies."

Writing Phase:

1. Organization
    - Historical context
    - Current research
    - Competing viewpoints
    - Synthesis of findings
    - Recommended solutions

2. Source Integration
   - Direct quotes
   - Statistical evidence
   - Expert testimony
   - Case studies

Skills Developed:
- Advanced research
- Complex synthesis
- Academic writing
- Scholarly conventions

Supporting the Progression

Mentors can support this development by:

1. Meeting Students Where They Are

   - Identify current writing level
   - Build on existing strengths
   - Address specific challenges
   - Provide appropriate challenges

2. Offering Strategic Support

   - Model thinking processes
   - Teach research methods
   - Guide organization
   - Demonstrate revision

3. Maintaining High Standards

   - Set clear expectations
   - Provide specific feedback
   - Celebrate progress

- Encourage excellence

Remember: This progression isn't strictly linear. Students might work at different levels simultaneously depending on the task and topic. The key is providing appropriate support while maintaining high expectations for growth.

Supporting Student Growth

Understanding Writing Challenges

Writing challenges often run deeper than surface-level struggles with grammar or organization. Like an iceberg, visible difficulties frequently mask deeper issues that require understanding and targeted support.

What appears as "writer's block" often reflects deeper challenges that students face in their writing journeys. Some students struggle with overwhelming ideas, finding themselves paralyzed by having "too many thoughts at once." They may feel an insurmountable gap between their rich internal thoughts and their ability to express these ideas in writing, and their fear of imperfect expression may lead to complete paralysis. Conversely, other students experience what might be called "empty mind syndrome," where facing a blank page creates intense anxiety. This can be triggered by previous negative writing experiences, leading to a mental shutdown. In these cases, an overwhelming internal critic can effectively block any creative flow, making it impossible to begin writing at all.

<u>Support Strategies:</u>
1. Begin with verbal expression

2. Use brainstorming techniques

3. Start with short, manageable writing tasks

4. Provide structured prompts when needed

5. Celebrate small successes

Learning Differences: Alternate Paths to Expression

Students with learning differences like dyslexia or dysgraphia require creative approaches that honor their unique thinking styles while supporting their growth as writers.

Example Adaptations:
- Voice recording thoughts before writing
- Using speech-to-text technology
- Creating visual outlines or mind maps
- Breaking tasks into smaller steps
- Allowing extra time for processing

<u>Success Story</u>: Alex, a student with dysgraphia, struggled with physical writing but had brilliant ideas. His mentor helped him:

1. Record initial thoughts verbally

2. Create visual story maps

3. Dictate first drafts

4. Gradually transition to typing

5. Focus on content before mechanics

Effective Mentoring Strategies

Meeting students where they are requires a thoughtful and comprehensive approach to assessment and planning. Mentors must first assess current abilities without judgment, creating a clear picture of where each student stands in their writing journey. Through careful observation and interaction, mentors identify specific challenges and strengths, using these insights to create individualized development plans that address each student's unique needs. By building on existing interests and passions, mentors keep students engaged and motivated in their writing development. Throughout this process, mentors maintain high expectations while providing the necessary support to help students reach their full potential.

Providing Constructive Feedback

The "Sandwich" approach provides a balanced framework for delivering feedback, but should only be implemented once students have progressed beyond the Practice Scholar phase and developed confidence in their writing voice. Introducing this structured critique too early risks stifling a student's emerging expression. However, once students have established their voice through Practice Scholar experiences, this three-layered approach can help mentors provide guidance that maintains student confidence while promoting growth. By structuring feedback in three distinct layers, mentors can ensure their critique is received as supportive guidance rather than discouraging criticism.

1. Begin with specific positive observations

    ▪ "Your description of the sunset really helped me see it clearly."

2. Offer targeted suggestions for improvement

    ▪ "Consider adding more sensory details in the second paragraph."

3. End with encouraging future focus

    ▪ "I'm excited to see how you develop this scene further."

<u>Key Principles:</u>

When providing guidance to students, it's important to maintain a focused and supportive approach. Mentors should concentrate on only one or two areas of improvement at a time to avoid overwhelming students, while providing specific examples that clearly illustrate the concepts being taught. By suggesting concrete next steps, mentors give students clear direction for moving forward in their development. Throughout this process, maintaining an encouraging tone helps students stay motivated and confident in their abilities. Regular celebration of progress, no matter how small, reinforces positive growth and keeps students engaged in their learning journey.

Setting the Stage for Success

The setting in which writing occurs profoundly impacts both

the process and its outcomes. Like a garden that requires the right conditions for growth, writers need carefully cultivated spaces that nurture their development. A well-designed writing setting offers quiet areas for concentration, readily available resources, and comfortable seating with good lighting. Minimizing distractions, from noise to visual clutter, helps maintain the focused attention that deep writing requires.

Even more crucial is the emotional setting we create around writing. Students need to feel safe sharing their thoughts without fear of harsh judgment. This safety emerges from consistently demonstrating respect for all voices, regardless of their current level of development. The celebration of progress plays a vital role, with mentors acknowledging small steps forward rather than focusing solely on final products.

Regular writing routines help establish this supportive setting. Setting aside specific times for writing, creating predictable patterns for sharing and feedback, and maintaining consistent expectations all contribute to a setting where writers feel secure enough to take creative risks. Through these carefully crafted physical and emotional settings, authentic voice and refined craft can flourish together.

The Parent Partnership

When you are mentoring children other than your own, clear communication with parents forms a crucial foundation for successful writing development. Like building a strong bridge, creating effective parent partnerships requires careful attention to both structure and connection. Parents need to understand not just what we're doing but why we're taking this approach, particularly regarding how voice development precedes technical precision—much like a child learns to speak before mastering grammar.

Consider how one mentor handled concerns with Jamie's mother, who worried about grammar mistakes in her daughter's writing. Rather than dismissing these concerns, the mentor explained the focus on voice development and shared specific strategies for supporting writing at home, such as engaging in conversations about ideas before writing and responding first to content rather than corrections. Through regular progress updates, the mentor kept Jamie's mother informed while celebrating her daughter's growing confidence as a writer.

Parents need to understand that writing growth, like physical growth, happens gradually and sometimes unevenly. When they understand and support our approach to writing development, they can reinforce these principles at home, creating a consistent and encouraging environment for their children's growth as writers. Regular communication, whether through scheduled conferences or informal updates, ensures everyone remains aligned in supporting the student's development.

Writing as a Transformative Force

Let's return to Julie, whose grandmother's immigration story was buried under red ink. Imagine instead if her teacher had responded first to the power of her narrative, helping her strengthen her grandmother's voice while gradually developing the technical skills to polish her work. This approach—honoring voice while building craft—represents the heart of writing in LEMI's Writing Philosophy.

Writing development, like climbing a mountain, happens one step at time. From speaking to writing, from personal expression to academic discourse, from opinion to research—each stage builds upon previous ones, creating not just better writers but more thoughtful, articulate individuals. As one mentor observed, "We're not teaching students to write perfectly; we're teaching them to write powerfully." This power emerges from the combination of authentic voice and developed skill.

Effective mentors maintain crucial balances: voice and technique, creativity and structure, freedom and guidance. They honor the natural progression of writing development while creating safe spaces for growth. Most importantly, they keep sight of writing's larger purpose—developing individuals who can think deeply, express clearly, and lead effectively.

When we approach writing as a transformative force rather than merely a technical skill, the impact extends far beyond the classroom. Students discover their voices, ideas find powerful expression, and communities gain articulate leaders. Through patient mentoring that honors both voice and craft, we help students discover writing not as a burden to bear but as a powerful tool for personal growth and meaningful impact.

Remember: Every writer's journey is unique. Our role as mentors is not to create a single path but to guide each student in finding their own way forward, supporting them as they develop both the confidence to speak and the skill to be heard. In doing so, we help develop not just better writers but more capable leaders ready to make their unique contributions to the world.

While writing provides a foundational tool for developing and expressing ideas, students often need individualized guidance to deepen their understanding and refine their skills. This brings us to our next learning environment: tutorials. Through focused, personalized interactions between mentor and student, tutorials create intimate spaces where writing and other academic skills can be carefully cultivated. As we'll explore in the next chapter, these small group sessions offer unique opportunities for both targeted instruction and collaborative discovery, complementing and enhancing the broader work of writing development.

Let's Take a Deeper Look — Chapter 9

These questions aren't just for pondering – they're invitations to connect these ideas with your own journey and vision as an educator. Take time to explore them deeply, perhaps journaling your thoughts or discussing them with fellow mentors.

1. The chapter contrasts Julie's experience of harsh criticism with a more nurturing approach to writing development. Reflect on your own experiences with writing feedback – both receiving and giving it. How have these experiences shaped your approach to mentoring writers? What elements of effective feedback would you want to incorporate into your practice?

2. Consider the LEMI Writing Cycle described in the chapter (from Listening through Research). How might understanding this progression change how you approach writing instruction? Think of a specific student. Where are they in this cycle and what support might they need to progress naturally to the next stage?

3. The chapter emphasizes the importance of allowing voice to emerge before focusing on mechanics. What challenges might you face in implementing this approach, particularly if you're working within a traditional educational system? How could you balance nurturing authentic expression while still developing necessary technical skills?

4. The chapter discusses developing writers across different phases (Discovery through Scholar Phase). Choose one phase that you currently work with or plan to work with. What specific strategies from the chapter could you implement to better support writers in this phase? What adaptations might you need to make for your specific context?

5. Think about the concept of "Writing as Discovery" presented in the chapter. When have you experienced writing as a tool for clarifying your own thoughts? How might you create opportunities for your students to experience this transformative aspect of writing?

Resources for Deeper Learning:

LEMIWorks! Podcast Classic Call episodes "Writing-Part 1" and "Writing-Part 2" available at LEMIWorks.com[6]

LEMI Writing Seminar - find more information on LEMI-U.com/Support/

LEMI Mentor Training - a three day immersive program where participants are trained in project-based learning, Leadership Education and the Learning Environments. For more information go to LEMIHomeschool.com

CHAPTER 10

Tutorial:
Facilitating Deeper Understanding
Through Collaborative Learning

Mary noticed her scholar students seemed stuck. Two weeks after receiving their project assignments, their journals remained empty, and class discussions revealed more uncertainty than excitement.

She invited her six students to an optional tutorial session in the library, asking them to bring any ideas they had—even incomplete ones. Creating an informal atmosphere with comfortable chairs arranged in a circle, Mary turned to Michael, who had been particularly quiet. "What's bouncing around in your head?"

"I'm interested in sound waves and music, but it feels too vague. I don't know where to start," Michael admitted.

"That reminds me of that video about dolphins using sound waves," Emma offered. "What if you explored underwater acoustics?"

Michael's eyes lit up. "I've always wondered how whales communicate over long distances..."

The conversation flowed from there. Each student shared early ideas while others offered suggestions. Jessica's interest in photography evolved into exploring early photographic processes, while Tyler's passion for basketball led to investigating the physics of rubber.

By the session's end, every student had a clearer direction, and their peers contributed research questions. Their initial anxiety had transformed into enthusiasm, demonstrating how a small group tutorial could turn uncertainty into focused purpose.

Understanding Tutorials

A tutorial is more than just a small group discussion; it's a carefully orchestrated session drawing inspiration from the centuries-old Oxford Tutorial model, where learning happens through intimate intellectual discourse between tutor and students. At Oxford tutorials typically involve a tutor meeting with just two or three students for about an hour of focused discussion about their prepared work. Unlike traditional classroom settings, tutorials create an environment where each participant actively contributes to the learning process, functioning as both learner and teacher.[1] The mentor's role shifts from instructor to facilitator, guiding students to delve deeper into the material and challenge each others' understanding. This approach creates an environment of rigorous but supportive academic engagement, where students learn to articulate and defend their ideas, respond thoughtfully to criticism, and develop independent thinking skills. Through tutorials, students develop crucial abilities including:

- Critical analysis and deep engagement with content

- Articulation and defense of ideas
- Active listening and thoughtful response
- Constructive feedback and peer review
- Intellectual risk-taking and growth

The success of a tutorial depends on all participants understanding and fulfilling their roles. Students must prepare thoroughly beforehand, complete assigned readings or tasks, engage deeply with the material, and come ready to contribute meaningfully to discussions. The mentor guides the conversation, asks probing questions, and ensures balanced participation while maintaining focus on the learning objectives.

Creating Effective Tutorial Environments

The transformative power of tutorials emerges when mentors successfully cultivate an atmosphere of mutual respect and intellectual curiosity. This environment should:

1. **Support Intellectual Risk-Taking**

   - Encourage the sharing of incomplete ideas
   - Welcome questions and exploration
   - Value process as much as conclusions

2. **Focus on Student Work**

   - Center discussions around student-created content
   - Use essays, research projects, or personal reflections as starting points
   - Provide opportunities for presenting and defending ideas

3. **Foster Deep Learning**

   - Move beyond surface understanding
   - Make connections across subjects and ideas
   - Encourage the application of concepts to new situations

Tutorials often lead to profound "aha" moments as students grapple with complex ideas, receive feedback, and refine their thinking. These breakthrough moments of understanding become hallmarks of effective tutorial experiences.

Practical Implementation

When to Use Tutorials

Mentors must develop a keen eye for recognizing when tutorials best serve their students' needs. The need for tutorials often becomes apparent in several situations:

- When students struggle with specific concepts requiring individualized attention
- During complex projects demanding sustained guidance
- When students show high interest but need structured direction
- For challenging material requiring close analysis and discussion
- To help establish effective scholarly habits

Remember that tutorials work best as bridges to independence, not permanent supports. The goal is to develop students' skills and confidence for effective independent work.

Structure and Organization

Structure and Organization require thoughtful planning and consistent documentation to ensure effective tutorials. Before each session, mentors must carefully plan by setting clear objectives that guide the interaction. This preparation includes reviewing student work beforehand to identify specific areas needing attention and gathering relevant resources that might support the learning process. Developing guiding questions helps maintain focus and stimulates productive discussion during the tutorial. Sessions should be scheduled for 30-60 minutes, providing enough time for meaningful interaction without overwhelming participants. While maintaining regular meeting times creates a helpful routine, mentors should remain flexible enough to accommodate urgent needs that may arise.

Documentation plays a crucial role in the tutorial process. Mentors should systematically track both progress and challenges, creating a record that helps identify patterns and growth over time. Recording key insights and breakthroughs during sessions captures valuable learning moments and helps inform future interactions. It's essential to document agreed-upon next steps, ensuring both mentor and student have a clear direction for moving forward. Maintaining organized resource records helps build a library of effective materials and strategies that can be referenced and shared as needed.

Tutorial Applications

Writing Development

One-on-one or small group tutorials prove especially valuable when students begin major writing projects. These sessions allow mentors to:

- Guide research methodology
- Review outlines and drafts
- Work through argumentation challenges
- Teach citation methods
- Provide immediate feedback

For example, in the LEMI Civil War project, Sword of Freedom, students write a "Hero Report" – often their first formal research paper. This assignment requires them to research a historical figure, document sources, and write a detailed analysis. Tutorials prove invaluable during this process, allowing mentors to guide students through research strategies, source evaluation, and proper citation methods. Through focused tutorial sessions, students develop the research and writing skills they'll need throughout their scholarly careers while receiving the personalized support needed for this significant academic milestone.

Complex Text Analysis

When tackling challenging classical works, small group

tutorials (3-4 students) help students:

- Break down difficult passages
- Explore various interpretations
- Connect ideas across texts and to contemporary issues
- Develop critical reading techniques
- Build analytical skills through collaboration

For example, in the LEMI Shakespeare Conquest project, students must master complex Elizabethan English as they prepare to perform a Shakespeare play. Tutorials offer a safe space to work through challenging passages together. A mentor might guide 2-3 students through close reading of their lines, helping them unpack unfamiliar vocabulary, explore the deeper meanings behind the words, and understand their character's motivations. These focused sessions transform potentially frustrating text into accessible, meaningful dialogue that students can perform with confidence and understanding.

Project Development

Regular tutorial meetings provide essential support for independent research or creative projects by:

- Reviewing progress and challenges
- Discussing methodology and next steps
- Providing resources and guidance
- Helping refine ideas
- Maintaining momentum through accountability

For example, in the LEMI Edison Project, self-directed scholars design and execute their own in-depth projects.

Tutorial: Facilitating Deeper Understanding

During this challenging process, tutorials become essential checkpoints for success. A mentor might meet with a small group of students to help refine their initial project scope, brainstorm research approaches, or work through specific obstacles. These focused meetings help scholars develop both their project and crucial self-directed learning skills.

The Lasting Impact of Effective Tutorials

Tutorials transcend simple information transfer, becoming powerful environments for cultivating critical thinking, meaningful application, intellectual curiosity, and independent learning. When executed effectively, they prepare students not just for academic success but for lifelong engagement with ideas and effective leadership. The intimate nature of tutorials, combined with their focus on active learning and personal growth, makes them an invaluable tool in Leadership Education.

While tutorials excel at fostering deep understanding through collaborative learning, sometimes students need even more individualized attention to master specific skills. This is where coaching, our next learning environment, becomes essential. Like tutorials, coaching provides focused guidance but with an emphasis on developing particular abilities through systematic practice and feedback. As we'll explore in the next chapter, the art of coaching adds another vital dimension to our mentoring toolkit.

Let's Take a Deeper Look – Chapter 10

These questions aren't just for pondering – they're invitations to connect these ideas with your own journey and vision as an educator. Take time to explore them deeply, perhaps journaling your thoughts or discussing them with fellow mentors.

1. Think about a time when you participated in a small group learning experience. How did it compare to the tutorial model described in this chapter? What elements made it effective or ineffective?

2. Reflect on the dual role of students as both learners and teachers in a tutorial setting. How does this approach differ from traditional education models? What benefits and challenges do you see in this method?

3. Consider the mentor's role in a tutorial. How does it differ from the role of a traditional teacher? If you're a mentor, how might you adapt your approach to better facilitate a tutorial-style learning environment?

4. How do you think the skills developed in a tutorial setting (critical thinking, articulating ideas, giving and receiving feedback) translate to leadership roles? Can you think of specific ways these skills might be applied in real-world leadership situations?

Resources for Deeper Learning:

Supercharge Your Mentoring Seminar –a transformative two-day workshop designed to elevate your mentoring skills. Led by an experienced LEMI trainer, you'll collaborate with peers to craft an engaging experience for youth on the second day. More information can be found at LEMI-U.com/ Support

CHAPTER 11

Coaching:
Nurturing Growth Through
Personalized Guidance

John stared at his copy of *A Midsummer Night's Dream*[1], hands trembling. Playing Lysander in three weeks seemed impossible—the Elizabethan English felt like a foreign language, and his voice barely carried past the first row.

"I can't do this," he confided to his mentor, Kathy. "Maybe someone else should take the role."

Rather than offering solutions, Kathy had John stand and physically act out Lysander's determination. With each stride across the room, his voice grew stronger. The words that had seemed foreign began to flow naturally, powered by the movement.

Through targeted coaching sessions over the next weeks, Kathy helped John break down each scene into manageable pieces. They developed specific techniques for projection, emotional expression, and memorization, building on what worked best for his learning style.

By opening night, John had found not only Lysander's voice but his own. His journey from hesitation to confidence exemplifies the power of coaching in Leadership Education, where personalized guidance transforms challenges into achievable steps toward mastery.

While traditionally associated with sports or music, coaching extends far beyond, encompassing academic pursuits and personal development. This versatile learning environment supports the mastery of both practical skills and targeted abilities.

The Core Elements of Coaching

At its heart, coaching is about guiding students through the process of mastering specific skills or abilities. What distinguishes coaching from other learning environments is its highly personalized, iterative nature. Whether developing tangible skills like essay writing or abilities like time management, coaching provides targeted support for individual growth.

The Coaching Cycle

The foundation of effective coaching lies in its systematic approach to improvement:

1. **Attempt:** The student practices the skill or completes the task

2. **Feedback:** The coach provides specific, constructive guidance

3. **Refinement:** The student incorporates feedback and tries again

This cycle continues, with each iteration bringing the student closer to mastery. Crucially, failure becomes not a setback but a valuable source of learning. Skilled coaches help students extract lessons from every attempt, transforming challenges into stepping stones toward success.

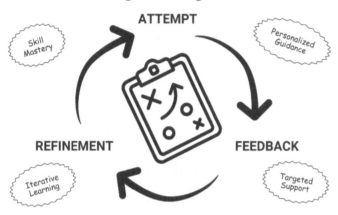

The Coaching Learning Environment

ATTEMPT

Skill Mastery

Personalized Guidance

REFINEMENT

FEEDBACK

Iterative Learning

Targeted Support

The Power of Incremental Progress

Coaching excels through its focus on gradual improvement. Each attempt builds upon previous efforts, with coaches providing targeted advice for specific areas of difficulty. This approach makes even complex skills manageable by breaking them down into achievable steps, steadily building both competence and confidence.

Building Character Through Coaching

While skill development remains central, effective coaching nurtures both ability and character. Through thoughtful guidance and encouragement, coaches help students develop:

- A growth mindset
- Resilience
- Determination
- Self-belief
- Personal self-awareness

For example, when a coach says, "I know you can master this; I've seen you overcome even greater challenges," they reinforce the student's capacity for growth and perseverance. Such affirmations shape students' self-perception and approach to future challenges.

Practical Application Examples

The power of coaching becomes evident in several key areas of LEMI projects:

Shakespeare Performance Coaching

In LEMI's Shakespeare Conquest, coaching transforms students from hesitant readers of complex text into confident performers. One-on-one coaching sessions help students:

- Master pronunciation of Early Modern English
- Develop their character's motivations and personality
- Build stage presence and projection skills
- Gain confidence in memorization and delivery

Each coaching session focuses on specific aspects of performance, allowing students to progress from understanding their lines to embodying their characters.

Writing Mentoring

Writing mentoring, as a form of one-on-one coaching, threads through all LEMI projects, with each project presenting unique challenges. Mentors guide students through:

- Finding their voice by guiding them to hear their thought
- Crafting clear thesis statements and arguments
- Developing research methodologies
- Structuring effective paragraphs and transitions
- Refining flow and lines of logic

Through mentors' comments on papers, students receive feedback on their work and specific strategies for improvement. This personalized guidance helps them develop from finding their voice and basic writing skills to scholarly expression.

Public Speaking in QUEST

QUEST, a LEMI project for Apprentice Scholars, has several months where students focus on their public speaking skills. Coaching sessions help students:

- Build logical arguments
- Develop confident delivery
- Master improvisational responses
- Handle challenging questions effectively

Mentors work individually with students, progressing from

basic speech preparation to advanced legal argumentation. Through repeated practice and feedback cycles, students develop the poise and precision needed for these demanding presentations.

In each application, coaching provides the structured support and personalized guidance students need to master complex skills while building confidence and competence.

Creating a Vision and Environment for Growth

Great coaches understand that their role extends beyond teaching specific skills to helping students envision their broader potential. By connecting current learning to future applications, coaches help students see how each skill they master contributes to their larger educational journey and life aspirations. This vision-casting transforms seemingly isolated tasks into meaningful steps toward significant goals. Students begin to recognize how mastering a particular skill—whether public speaking, writing, or analytical thinking—develops transferable abilities that will serve them well beyond the immediate context.

Creating this expansive vision requires an environment where students feel safe to take risks and push beyond their comfort zones. The foundation of such an environment is trust between coach and student, built through consistent, constructive feedback and genuine care for the student's growth. In this atmosphere, mistakes are not viewed as failures but as natural steps in the learning process. Coaches celebrate effort and progress, knowing that acknowledgment of small victories builds the confidence needed for tackling bigger challenges.

When students understand how their current work connects to their future potential and feel secure in taking the risks necessary for growth, they develop not just competence but confidence. They begin to see themselves as capable of continuous learning and improvement, embracing challenges rather than avoiding them. This combination of clear vision and a supportive environment enables students to progress steadily toward mastery while developing the resilience and self-belief essential for leadership.

Transforming Lives One Student at a Time

The coaching environment transforms students through personalized guidance, systematic practice, and encouraging support. It develops not just specific skills but confident, resilient learners ready for ongoing growth and challenge.

While coaching excels at providing individualized guidance, there are times when broader knowledge needs to be shared with larger groups. This brings us to our next learning environment: the lecture. Through carefully crafted presentations and engaging delivery, lectures can inspire and inform multiple students simultaneously, complementing the personalized attention of coaching with efficient transmission of foundational knowledge and key insights.

Let's Take a Deeper Look – Chapter 11

These questions aren't just for pondering – they're invitations to connect these ideas with your own journey and vision as an educator. Take time to explore them deeply, perhaps journaling your thoughts or discussing them with fellow mentors.

1. Think about a time when you were coached effectively, either in an academic, professional, or personal context. What specific strategies did the coach use that made the experience impactful? How can you apply these strategies in your own role as a mentor or learner?

2. Consider the concept of viewing failure as an integral part of the learning process. How might this perspective change your approach to learning new skills or facing challenges? Can you think of a personal example where reframing a failure as a learning opportunity would have been beneficial?

3. The chapter emphasizes the importance of incremental progress. Think of a complex skill you've mastered or are currently learning. How can you break it down into smaller, manageable steps? How might this approach affect your motivation and confidence?

4. Consider the power of encouragement and vision-casting in coaching. Can you recall a time when someone's belief in your abilities significantly impacted

your performance or self-perception? How can you incorporate more intentional encouragement in your interactions with others?

5. The chapter suggests that effective coaching goes beyond skill development to nurture mindset and character. What character traits do you think are most important to develop through coaching? How might you focus on cultivating these traits in yourself or others?

Resources for Deeper Learning:

> **Unleashing Your Voice**–A dynamic two-day workshop where you'll witness an experienced LEMI trainer coaching youth in speech and debate on day one. On day two, it's your turn to step into the spotlight and experience the power of being coached firsthand. Find more information at LEMI-U.com/Support.

CHAPTER 12

Lectures:
Transforming Information into Inspiration

In Jane Austen's *Pride and Prejudice*, Mr. Collins reads a sermon with such "monotonous solemnity" that he leave his audience uninspired, while Mr. Bennet's informal but insightful conversations captivate his daughter Elizabeth's attention through wit and relevant connections. [1] This contrast illustrates the difference between mere information delivery and effective lecturing.

While formal lectures are often overused and can stifle active learning, when employed strategically, they remain powerful tools for imparting new information and insights. Like Mr. Bennet, effective lecturers do more than transmit information—they engage their audience's minds and hearts, connecting new knowledge to existing understanding.

The key lies in understanding when and how to use lectures within the broader landscape of Leadership Education. A well-crafted lecture can illuminate complex concepts, provide context for deeper study, and inspire independent learning. This requires moving beyond passive information reception to create "engaging lectures" that combine clear instruction with interaction, reflection, and connection to students' lives.

This chapter explores how to create and deliver presentations that not only inform but also inspire and transform, examining the elements that distinguish powerful lectures from mere information delivery, and providing practical guidance for when and how to use this impactful learning environment.

Understanding the Lecture Environment

A lecture is essentially a structured presentation of information by an educator or invited expert to a group of listeners. It typically involves careful preparation, with the presenter either reading from a prepared text or speaking from a detailed outline. The key to a successful lecture lies in understanding your audience, gauging their attention span, and maintaining their interest throughout the presentation.

Types of Lectures

Formal Lectures are delivered from a written text by subject matter experts, with questions typically reserved for the end. These lectures benefit students by providing structured, comprehensive overviews of topics while ensuring logical coverage of key points. They excel at presenting complex information precisely and creating valuable reference materials for future use. To maximize effectiveness, speakers should prepare clear scripts, practice engaging delivery despite reading from the text, use supporting visuals, offer periodic summaries, and provide handouts. Adequate time for questions at the conclusion is essential. This type of lecture is more appropriate for older students who have longer attention spans. Use sparingly, if at all, for Practice Scholar or Discovery Phase students.

Informal Lectures follow an outline format and welcome interaction throughout the presentation. Their strength lies in encouraging active participation, allowing real-time clarification, and building personal connections between speaker and audience. This format adapts readily to audience needs and facilitates deeper understanding through dialogue. Successful informal lectures require detailed but flexible outlines, frequent discussion opportunities, real-world examples, and thought-provoking questions that, when asked intermittently throughout the lecture, can allow students to break into smaller groups and share their own insights on the topic and question, bringing relevance and a shared experience. Speakers should be prepared to adjust their presentation based on audience response and encourage participant sharing. Informal lectures can be effective across all phases of learning, with the level of interactivity adjusted to match student development—younger students benefit from shorter segments with frequent interaction, while scholar phase students can engage with longer periods of content delivery interspersed with meaningful discussion.

Workshops blend lecture content with hands-on activities, creating an interactive learning environment. This format promotes active learning, enhances retention through practice, and allows participants to learn from both instructors and peers. Workshops effectively bridge theory and application through immediate practice. For best results, begin with a brief introductory lecture, design relevant activities, provide clear instructions, and conclude with a debrief session. Include varied activities to accommodate different learning styles and ensure time for group discussion and feedback. Like informal lectures, workshops can be adapted for all phases—shorter, game-based activities work well for Discovery Phase students, while Scholar Phase students can tackle more complex, extended projects and discussions.

Each lecture type serves a distinct purpose. Success depends on choosing the format that best aligns with your educational goals, audience needs, and subject matter.

Preparing Effective Lectures

The preparation process is crucial for delivering impactful lectures:

1. Content Gathering: Review existing notes, research new sources, and brainstorm freely to develop fresh insights.

2. Organization: Create a clear outline based on what you want your students to know, feel, and ultimately do, connecting your points logically and including attention-grabbing elements and illustrative stories.

3. Know Your Audience: Tailor your content and delivery to your listeners' level of understanding and interests.

Key Principles for Effective Lectures

Effective lectures combine five classical rhetorical elements to create engaging, memorable learning experiences:

1. **Ethos (Credibility)**[2]

   - Demonstrate expertise through depth of knowledge
   - Build trust by acknowledging the limits of understanding
   - Share relevant experiences that highlight the topic connection
   - Use and cite credible sources appropriately

2. **Pathos (Passion)**[3]

   - Share authentic enthusiasm for your subject
   - Use vivid language and compelling stories
   - Connect content to audience experiences
   - Create a positive emotional atmosphere with appropriate humor

3. **Logos (Logic)**[4]

   - Present information in a clear, logical sequence
   - Support points with evidence and examples
   - Explain complex ideas step-by-step
   - Use analogies to clarify difficult concepts

4. **Taxis (Organization)**[5]

   - Begin with an attention-grabbing introduction
   - Present main points in coherent order
   - Use clear transitions between sections
   - End with a memorable conclusion
   - Include signposts to guide the audience

5. **Lexis (Language)**[6]

- Use clear, concise language
- Explain technical terms when necessary
- Employ descriptive language for engagement
- Vary sentence structure for interest
- Adapt vocabulary to audience level

5 Elements of Effective Lectures

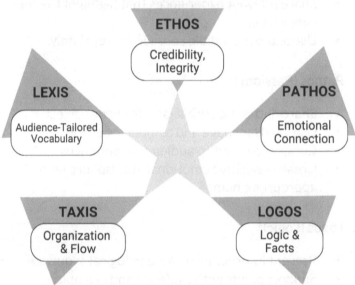

These principles work together to create lectures that inform, inspire, and motivate students. By mastering these elements, mentors demonstrate effective communication while developing future leaders.

Creating Dynamic Lectures: Keys to Audience Engagement

Master these seven techniques to transform passive listeners into active participants:

1. **Master the Art of Storytelling.** Stories captivate minds and make information memorable. Choose narratives that clearly illustrate key points, drawing from both personal experience and well-known examples. Craft each story with a clear beginning, middle, and end, ensuring it serves your educational purpose.

2. **Connect Through Eye Contact.** Scan the room systematically, making brief but meaningful eye contact with your audience. Use these connections to gauge understanding and adjust your presentation accordingly. Let your eyes reflect a genuine passion for the subject matter, as enthusiasm proves contagious.

3. **Harness the Power of Movement.** Move purposefully around the space, using deliberate gestures to emphasize key points. Approach the audience to create connection and intensity, then step back when you want them to reflect. Ensure each movement enhances rather than distracts from your message.

4. **Modulate Your Voice.** Vary your volume, pace, and tone strategically. Slow down for important points, speed up to maintain momentum, and use well-timed pauses for emphasis. Let your voice convey both information and emotion, helping students connect with the material.

5. **Encourage Active Participation.** Transform passive listeners into engaged participants by incorporating thought-provoking questions and brief discussions. Create opportunities for students to process and apply concepts through pair discussions or small group activities. Use these interactions to gauge comprehension and maintain interest.

6. **Share Personal Connections.** Demonstrate why the topic matters by sharing specific examples from your

own learning journey. Show how your understanding has evolved, modeling the learning process for your students. These authentic connections help bridge the gap between theory and application.

7. **Leverage Visual Aids.** Support your message with clear, relevant visuals that enhance understanding. Create uncluttered slides or demonstrations that complement rather than duplicate your spoken content. Use visual elements strategically to reinforce key concepts and accommodate different learning styles.

Remember, these techniques should enhance your content, not overshadow it. The goal is to create a dynamic experience that supports deep learning and retention while modeling effective leadership communication.

From Presentation to Practice

Effective lectures transform traditional information delivery into engaging learning experiences that inspire and motivate. Through careful attention to structure, engagement techniques, and dynamic delivery, mentors can create presentations that not only convey knowledge but model the communication skills essential for leadership.

However, even the most compelling lecture has limitations. Students need opportunities to apply and practice what they've learned. This is where simulations become invaluable. While lectures help students understand principles and concepts, simulations allow them to experience these ideas in action. Through carefully designed scenarios and role-playing experiences, students move from passive understanding to active engagement with the material.

In our next chapter, we'll explore how simulations create safe spaces for experimenting with new ideas, practicing skills, and developing the confidence needed for real-world application. By combining the foundational knowledge gained through lectures with the experiential learning of simulations, we create a powerful framework for developing capable, confident leaders.

Let's Take a Deeper Look – Chapter 12

These questions aren't just for pondering – they're invitations to connect these ideas with your own journey and vision as an educator. Take time to explore them deeply, perhaps journaling your thoughts or discussing them with fellow mentors.

1. Think about the most memorable lecture you've ever attended. What made it stand out? How did the speaker engage you, and how might you incorporate similar techniques into your own lectures?

2. Consider the three types of lectures discussed (formal, informal, and workshop). Which style do you feel most comfortable with, and why? How might you challenge yourself to incorporate elements from the other styles?

3. Reflect on the principle of ethos (credibility). How do you currently establish your credibility when speaking? Can you think of ways to improve this while also acknowledging and building upon your audience's existing knowledge?

4. Think about the engagement techniques discussed in the chapter. Which one do you think would be most impactful in your teaching context? How might you begin to implement it?

Resources for Deeper Learning:

> **Unleashing Your Voice–**A dynamic two-day workshop where you'll witness an experienced LEMI trainer coaching youth in speech and debate on day one. On day two, it's your turn to step into the spotlight and experience the power of being coached firsthand. Find more information at LEMI-U.com/Support.

> **LEMI Mentor Training** - a three day immersive program where participants are trained in project-based learning, Leadership Education and the Learning Environments. For more information go to LEMIHomeschool.com

CHAPTER 13

Simulations:
Bridging Theory and Practice

Imagine walking into a classroom transformed into the
Assembly Room of Philadelphia's Pennsylvania State House
in 1776. The mentor, now acting as John Hancock, President
of the Continental Congress, calls the delegates to order.
Around the room, students representing different colonies
wrestle with the momentous decision before them: whether
to declare independence from Great Britain. A delegate
from South Carolina passionately argues for removing
references to slavery from Jefferson's draft declaration,
while a representative from Massachusetts staunchly
defends the original language. The tension in the classroom
is palpable—not just because students are playing roles, but
because they're experiencing firsthand the complex
dynamics that shaped our nation's founding.

This scene from LEMI's Key of Liberty Scholar Project
illustrates the exciting power of simulations in education.
Students aren't merely reading about historical events;
they're living them. They're not just learning about the
compromises that forged the Declaration of Independence;
they're actively negotiating those compromises themselves,
feeling the weight of decisions that would affect millions of
lives.

The Continental Congress simulation demonstrates how

simulations can bridge the gap between theoretical understanding and practical wisdom. Students must:

- Understand their colony's specific interests and concerns
- Navigate complex political and moral dilemmas
- Practice the art of negotiation and compromise
- Experience the challenge of building consensus among diverse interests
- Confront difficult issues like slavery that the founders themselves struggled with

Through this immersive experience, abstract historical concepts become tangible realities. The philosophical principles discussed in class take on new meaning as students grapple with their practical application. When a student representing Georgia must decide whether to support independence from Britain despite their colony's dependence on British trade and slavery, they're not just memorizing historical facts; they're developing a deeper understanding of the human dynamics that drive historical events.

This chapter explores how simulations like the Continental Congress Simulation create powerful learning environments that develop critical thinking, emotional intelligence, and leadership capabilities. We'll examine the essential elements that make simulations effective, discuss various types of simulations and their applications, and provide practical guidance for designing and implementing these learning experiences.

Whether you're a mentor planning your first simulation or an experienced educator looking to enhance your existing programs, understanding the principles and practices of effective simulations can help you create engaging, meaningful learning experiences that bridge the gap between theory and practice, between past and present, between knowledge and wisdom.

Core Elements of Effective Simulations

Essential Components

The Continental Congress Simulation in Key of Liberty provides an excellent framework for understanding the critical components that make simulations effective learning environments. Let's examine each essential element through this lens:

1. Clear Learning Objectives – Every simulation must begin with well-defined learning goals. In the Continental Congress simulation, these included:

- Understanding the complex factors that led to American independence
- Experiencing the challenges of building consensus among diverse interests
- Developing negotiation skills as well as knowing when to compromise for the greater good
- Gaining insight into the moral and practical dilemmas of the founding era
- Learning to articulate and defend positions based on evidence

2. Engaging Scenario/Narrative – The scenario must capture students' imagination and be meaningful. The Continental Congress simulation achieves this by:

- Setting a clear historical context (Philadelphia, Summer 1776)
- Creating dramatic tension (the decision for independence)
- Providing compelling personal stakes (representing colony interests)
- Including moral dilemmas (slavery, loyalty to Britain, economic interests)
- Building toward a significant culminating event (signing the Declaration)

3 Time Management Structure – The simulation needs a clear timeline:

- Opening context and role assignment
- Initial debate on independence
- Review and editing of the Declaration draft
- Final debate and voting
- Signing ceremony (if approved)
- Debriefing session

4. Debriefing Plan – A structured reflection process helps students process and internalize their learning

- Seek to understand emotional responses
- Connections to historical events
- Analysis of key decisions and their implications
- Personal insights and discoveries
- Applications to modern leadership challenges

5. Emotional and Physical Boundaries – Define the physical boundaries of the simulations; for instance, it might just be in the classroom, or it could take up several classrooms and the gym. Maybe it is outside at a campground and the students need to know the physical boundaries of where they are or are not allowed to go. Mentors should also be aware of any emotional boundaries that need to be set so that though challenges can be overcome, no one is abused or pushed too far.

By carefully attending to each of these components, mentors create an environment where students can safely explore complex situations while developing crucial leadership skills. The structure provides enough guidance to ensure meaningful learning while allowing sufficient flexibility for authentic interaction and discovery.

Remember, these components work together as an integrated system. The Continental Congress Simulation succeeds because each element has been carefully thought out, creating a comprehensive learning experience that engages students intellectually and emotionally while developing practical leadership skills.

Start with The "Know, Feel, Do" Framework in Simulation Design

The "Know, Feel, Do" framework guides mentors in designing purposeful simulations by answering three key questions:

1. Building Deep Understanding: What do I want my

students to know by the end of this lesson?

2. Creating Emotional Engagement: How can I help them to feel?

3. Inspiring Future Action: What do I want them to be inspired to do?

These questions help shape the direction of teaching and ensure the simulation has a clear purpose and impact. Let's explore how each element manifests in the Alien Planet Scenario, where students must negotiate survival in an unfamiliar world.

Implementation Example

Consider how these elements came together in a recent simulation where a student initially felt overwhelmed by their role as lead negotiator with the alien species. The mentor helped them focus on specific objectives:

Know:

- Basic principles of diplomatic exchange
- Resource requirements for group survival
- Cultural understanding protocols

Feel:

- Weight of responsibility for group survival
- Uncertainty of cross-cultural communication
- Connection with team members

Do:

- Develop and present negotiation strategies

- Build bridges across cultural differences
- Create sustainable agreements

Through this structured approach, the student not only learned negotiation principles but developed genuine empathy for cross-cultural communication challenges and practical skills in leadership and problem-solving.

The "Know, Feel, Do" framework ensures simulations move beyond simple role-playing to create deep, transformative learning experiences. In the Alien Planet Simulation, this comprehensive approach helps students develop not just strategic thinking skills but the emotional intelligence and practical capabilities essential for leadership in an increasingly interconnected world.

Types of Simulations and Their Applications

Different types of simulations serve unique learning purposes. Let's explore the five main categories and how they develop specific skills and capabilities.

Historical Reenactments

Historical reenactments transport students into pivotal moments of history, allowing them to experience and understand complex historical decisions firsthand.

Example: Nuremberg Trial (Found in LEMI's Hero Project)
Students step into the roles of litigators in prosecuting one of the Nazi war criminals. In this simulation, participants must thoroughly research historical evidence and testimony

while preparing compelling legal arguments to support their case. They learn to effectively cross-examine witnesses and present documentary evidence. Throughout the process, they develop the ability to argue complex moral and legal principles in a persuasive manner.

This type of simulation develops:

- Historical understanding
- Legal reasoning skills
- Public speaking abilities
- Ethical decision-making
- Understanding of justice and accountability

Futuristic Scenario Planning

Futuristic scenarios challenge students to apply problem-solving skills in unfamiliar contexts, forcing them to think creatively and strategically.

Example: Alien Negotiation Scenario – Students are stranded on an alien planet and must negotiate with the local species for survival. In this scenario, participants must work to establish communication with alien species while developing a deep understanding of their culture and customs. Students need to negotiate effectively for basic survival needs like food and shelter, carefully avoiding cultural misunderstandings that could threaten their safety. The ultimate goal is to create sustainable agreements with their alien hosts, all while ensuring they don't end up as the main course!

This develops:

- Creative problem-solving
- Cross-cultural communication
- Strategic thinking
- Risk assessment
- Adaptability

Crisis Management Exercises

These simulations place students under pressure to handle emergency situations, teaching rapid decision-making and team coordination.

Example: Alien Planet Crisis – Building on the previous scenario, students must navigate a range of sudden challenges that test their crisis management abilities. These include diplomatic breakdowns, critical resource shortages, and devastating natural disasters. They also face cultural misunderstandings that threaten their relationships, health emergencies that demand immediate response, and security threats that put their community at risk.

Students learn:

- Quick decision-making
- Team coordination
- Resource management
- Communication under pressure
- Priority setting

Physical Challenges

Physical challenges create tangible problems requiring teamwork, strategy, and creative thinking to solve.

Example: Crossing the Void – In this physical challenge, the entire class must work together to traverse a designated space called "the void" under specific constraints. They are given only a single small towel as a resource and must prevent any participant from touching the floor. The entire group needs to successfully cross within a limited time-frame while maintaining safety protocols, with mandatory participation from every student.

This develops:

- Team collaboration
- Strategic planning
- Physical coordination
- Problem-solving
- Leadership skills
- Group support

Role-Playing Exercises

Role-playing puts students into specific characters or positions, requiring them to understand and represent different perspectives. Role–playing can also help reinforce skills learning and ability development.

Example: Continental Congress Delegates – In the Key of Liberty simulation, students take on the roles of historical figures, maintaining consistent perspectives aligned with their assigned characters throughout the experience. They must convincingly argue positions based on their character's beliefs and motivations while building strategic alliances with other delegates. Each decision and interaction requires students to respond authentically from their character's historical viewpoint.

Role-playing develops:

- Perspective-taking
- Character consistency
- Public speaking
- Relationship building
- Ethical decision-making

Combining Simulation Types

Powerful learning often occurs when different types of simulations are combined. For example:

Historical + Role-Playing –The Continental Congress simulation combines historical accuracy with character embodiment.

Futuristic Scenario + Crisis Management – The Alien Planet scenario integrates long-term planning with immediate crisis response.

Physical + Team Building – The Crossing the Void challenge combines physical problem-solving with group dynamics.

Designing Simulations

Creating impactful simulations requires planning, skillful implementation, and thoughtful assessment. Let's explore each phase using our example simulations to illustrate effective design principles.

Planning Phase

1. Setting Clear Objectives

Use the "Know, Feel, Do" framework to establish specific goals. For example:

Alien Planet Negotiation Example:

- Know: Principles of diplomatic relations, cultural sensitivity, resource management
- Feel: Urgency of crisis, the importance of clear communication, the value of cooperation
- Do: Create strategic plans, navigate cultural differences, manage resources

2. Choosing Appropriate Simulation Type

Select based on your objectives. Consider combining types for richer experiences:

Historical Reenactment + Role-Play (Continental Congress):

- Maintains historical accuracy
- Allows character development
- Creates authentic conflicts
- Enables meaningful decisions

Futuristic Scenario + Crisis Management (Alien Planet):

- Encourages creative thinking
- Develops problem-solving skills
- Tests crisis response
- Builds team coordination

3. Creating Engaging Scenarios and Materials

Effective simulations need both well-crafted scenarios and carefully selected supporting materials. In the Continental Congress simulation, mentors prepare key scenario elements like historical context documents, parliamentary procedures, and delegate profiles, alongside practical materials such as fact sheets, nameplates, and voting guides. Similarly, the Alien Planet simulation requires a robust scenario foundation including planet descriptions, cultural guidelines, and resource limitations, supported by tangible materials like maps, tracking cards, and negotiation templates.

Keep materials streamlined and purposeful. They should enhance immersion while maintaining flexibility for organic learning to emerge. Each element should serve clear learning objectives rather than existing merely for atmospheric effect.

Implementation Guidelines

Successful simulation implementation requires careful attention to setup, facilitation, and ongoing management. Here's a comprehensive guide:

1. Setting Up the Environment

Create an immersive atmosphere that supports learning objectives. For example:

- Arrange physical space to match the simulation context (like the Assembly Hall for Continental

Congress)
- Provide necessary props and materials
- Establish clear boundaries for different activity zones
- Ensure safety measures are visible and accessible

2. Briefing and Launch

- Review objectives and expectations
- Explain rules clearly and concisely
- Define roles and responsibilities
- Address questions before beginning
- Establish safety protocols and boundaries

3. Managing the Experience

- Start small and build complexity gradually
- Monitor engagement and adjust as needed
- Support struggling participants while maintaining the challenge
- Look for and capitalize on teachable moments
- Document what works and what doesn't for future refinement

4. Maintaining Safety and Support

- Enforce physical safety protocols consistently
- Create emotional safety through respectful dialogue
- Provide modification options for different ability levels
- Monitor participants' comfort and engagement levels
- Have backup activities ready for unexpected situations

Remember that successful simulations can be simple while others can require more preparation and more materials.

Focus first on creating a safe, engaging environment where meaningful learning can occur, then gradually increase complexity as confidence and capability grow.

The Mentor's Role During Simulations

While careful planning is essential, the true art of facilitating simulations lies in knowing when to step back and let learning unfold organically. Like a director who must eventually trust their actors to bring a play to life, mentors need to resist the urge to control every aspect of the simulation once it begins.

Key Principles for Mentors During Simulations:

1. Create Space for Authentic Learning

   - Resist the urge to jump in and "fix" situations
   - Allow students to experience natural consequences of their choices
   - Step back physically to reduce the temptation to intervene
   - Trust the process even when it differs from your plan

2. Monitor Without Controlling

   - Maintain awareness of safety boundaries
   - Watch for signs of excessive frustration or conflict
   - Document key moments for later discussion
   - Allow productive struggle while preventing destructive conflict

3. Adapt to Emerging Situations

   - Be prepared to adjust time-frames as needed

Simulations: Bridging Theory & Practice

- Have backup plans but remain open to unexpected learning opportunities
- Follow the energy of the group when appropriate
- Remember that "failures" often provide the richest learning

4. Support Without Directing

- Offer clarification only when absolutely necessary
- Use questions rather than directions when intervention is needed
- Encourage students to find their own solutions
- Maintain safety protocols while allowing reasonable risk-taking

Remember: Some of the most powerful learning moments emerge when simulations don't go as planned. A simulation that seems to "fail" in the moment often provides rich material for debriefing and insight. Trust that the debrief will help students extract value from whatever unfolds.

When to Intervene:

- Physical safety concerns
- Emotional trauma risk
- Complete breakdown of simulation structure
- Clear violation of established boundaries

Otherwise, resist the urge to "perfect" the experience. The messiness of real interaction often creates the most authentic learning opportunities.

The Essential Role of Debriefing

Just as a well-designed simulation creates powerful learning experiences, effective debriefing transforms those experiences into lasting insights. Without thoughtful debriefing, even the most engaging simulation risks becoming merely an interesting activity rather than a transformative learning experience.

Every simulation debrief should include three essential elements:

1. Emotional Processing (5-10 minutes): Allow participants to process immediate reactions and feelings in a safe space. They can write about their emotions in a journal, or they can share with their neighbor or as a group.

   Sometimes students have to be reminded that the simulation part is over, and that they no longer need to stay in character or argue for their cause. Now is the time to reflect on what they experienced and learned, and to see what the others felt and learned as well.

2. Analysis (10-15 minutes): Examine key decisions, consequences, and learning moments.

3. Application (5-10 minutes): Connect experience to real-world applications and future actions.

For shorter simulations, you can focus on key questions like:

- What stood out to you about this experience?
- What did you learn about yourself or others?
- How might you use this learning going forward?
- Would you do anything differently next time?

If time is short remember, students can write about their experiences and/or share with their classmate.

For more on debriefing, see Chapter 14.

Simulations Across Different Learning Phases

Discovery Level (Ages 0-11)

At this level there are different kinds of simulations. For the young children, simulation is a good way of practicing a much needed behavior such as getting an adult's help instead of hitting, or practicing saying "please" or learning to share. Simulations are great ways of helping children practice kindness, thoughtfulness, thinking before acting, and other important life skills and character development.

Simulations at this age are also a great way to practice skills. Children's play is often full of simulations. They pretend to be teaching or to be baking or to be a mommy or daddy. Children's play is often a role-play or simulation. Maybe they are animals or robots or are flying to Mars on a rocket ship. Letting them create their own magical world of play is a great way for them to express themselves, to learn, and to practice what they see being modeled in their older siblings and family members.

For older children, simulations can include setting up physical challenges and simple role-playing. Keep rules simple and time frames short. At this age, simulations are excellent learning environments for teaching emotional regulation and making smart decisions. They can also introduce material, ideas, or give knowledge.

Example Simulations:

- Historical character dress-up and simple reenactments
- Basic team challenges like building a human bridge
- Role-playing behavior that aligns with moral values and integrity
- Nature exploration simulations
- Simple trade or marketplace games
- Basic storytelling role-play

When designing simulations for Discovery level students, mentors must prioritize clarity and engagement while maintaining an appropriate pace. Instructions should be straightforward and easily understood, with complex concepts broken down into manageable parts. Physical movement and interactive elements help maintain attention and enthusiasm, while frequent transitions prevent fatigue or loss of interest. The focus should remain on enjoying the learning process, with educational content woven naturally into engaging activities. Feedback should be immediate and concrete, helping students make clear connections between their actions and outcomes. Debriefing sessions at this level work best when kept brief and activity-based, incorporating drawing, movement, or simple group discussions to process the experience.

Practice Scholar Phase (Ages 12-14)

Practice Scholars can handle more complex simulations but still need clear structure and support. This is an excellent time to introduce historical reenactments and problem-solving scenarios.

Example Simulations:

- Simple historical reenactments
- Basic parliamentary procedures
- Team problem-solving challenges
- Beginning debate simulations
- Introduction to crisis management scenarios

Practice Scholar simulations require a thoughtful balance between providing structure and encouraging growing independence. Mentors should gradually introduce more complex rules and procedures, allowing students time to master each new element before adding additional complexity. This phase offers excellent opportunities for creative problem-solving, with students beginning to develop their own approaches to challenges while still having support available when needed. Peer feedback becomes increasingly valuable, helping students learn from each others' experiences and perspectives. Debriefing sessions can become more detailed, though they should remain focused and interactive to maintain engagement. Making explicit connections between simulation experiences and real-world applications helps students understand the relevance of their learning.

Apprentice Scholar Phase (Ages 14-16)

Apprentice Scholars are ready for simulations that are more complex. They can handle longer scenarios and more nuanced roles.

Example Simulations:

- Complex historical reenactments (Supreme Court Simulations)
- Detailed diplomatic scenarios
- Multi-session crisis management
- Advanced debate simulations
- Leadership challenge scenarios

Supporting Apprentice Scholars requires an approach that challenges students while maintaining appropriate scaffolding. Research becomes an integral component, with students taking responsibility for developing background knowledge and understanding their roles in depth. Strategic thinking should be emphasized, with students learning to consider long-term consequences and multiple perspectives in their decision-making. Extended role development allows for deeper engagement with characters or scenarios, while detailed debriefing sessions help students extract maximum learning from their experiences. Mentors should help students connect specific experiences to broader principles of leadership and human interaction. Independent preparation becomes increasingly important, with students taking greater responsibility for their readiness to participate.

Self-Directed Scholar Phase (Ages 16-18)

Students can handle more complex simulations and may even help design them. They're ready for scenarios that integrate multiple skills and concepts.

Example Simulations:

- Diplomatic negotiations
- Crisis management scenarios
- Student-designed historical reenactments
- Multi-phase leadership challenges
- Professional environment simulations

At the Self-Directed Scholar level, simulation design and implementation should reflect students' growing maturity and capability. Students can and should be involved in the design process, contributing ideas and helping refine scenarios to maximize learning opportunities. Ethical dilemmas can be more complex, requiring nuanced understanding and careful consideration of complex factors. Analysis and reflection should dive deep, with students examining not just what happened but why it happened and what broader principles are at play. Connections to future academic, professional, and personal applications become increasingly important as students prepare for life beyond their current educational experience. Leadership development takes center stage, with students practicing both leading and following in various contexts. Debriefing sessions can be extensive and multi-layered, incorporating individual reflection, group discussion, written analysis, and action planning for future application.

Simulation Types Across Learning Phases

Type	Discovery (0-11)	Practice Scholar (12-14)	Apprentice Scholar (14-16)	Self-Directed Scholar (16-18)
Historical	Simple role-play of historical figures; Basic historical games; Short character portrayals	Somewhat more complex simulations, Simple parliamentary procedures, and Basic historical scenes	Complex historical scenarios, Period-accurate debates, Extended character development	Student-designed historical reenactments; Multi-session historical scenarios; Leadership in complex historical simulations
Future Scenario	Basic problem-solving games; Simple "what if" scenarios; Guided exploration activities	Simple alien planet scenarios, Basic survival challenges, Introductory resource management	Complex diplomatic missions; Extended survival scenarios; Resource allocation challenges	Student-created future scenarios; Complex multi-variable challenges; Leadership in extended missions
Crisis	Simple emergency response games, Basic team challenges, Guided problem-solving	Basic disaster response; Simple community challenges; Introduction to decision-making	Complex emergency scenarios; Resource distribution challenges; Leadership under pressure	Design and lead crisis scenarios; Multi-phase emergency management; Complex stakeholder negotiations
Physical	Simple team activities, Basic cooperation games, Guided movement exercises	Team building exercises; Basic challenge courses; Simple group tasks	Complex physical challenges; Team leadership opportunities; Extended group projects	Design physical challenges; Lead team activities; Create new challenge scenarios
Role Playing	Simple character play, Basic storytelling roles, Guided dramatic play	Historical figure portrayals; Basic debate roles; Simple negotiation scenarios	Complex character development; Extended role maintenance; Leadership role practice	Create and lead role-play scenarios; Design complex simulations; Mentor younger students

Remember that these phases are guidelines, not rigid boundaries. Individual students may be ready for more or less complex simulations regardless of their age. The key is matching the simulation's complexity to students' developmental readiness while maintaining engagement and supporting growth.

Integrating Simulations into Project-Based Learning

Simulations are powerful components within project-based learning, providing immersive experiences that bridge theoretical understanding with practical application.

Effective integration supports skill development (communication, leadership, critical thinking) and character growth (emotional intelligence, confidence, integrity). The key is strategic timing – simulations should enhance rather than overshadow other project components.

When thoughtfully integrated, simulations transform traditional learning into experiential understanding, preparing students for real-world challenges while reinforcing project objectives.

From Experience to Understanding

Simulations are powerful tools that bridge the gap between theoretical understanding and practical wisdom. Through simulations, students develop not just knowledge but also the emotional intelligence, critical thinking, and leadership capabilities essential for navigating an increasingly complex world.

The success of simulations depends on clear learning objectives, age-appropriate design, attention to safety, and thoughtful integration with broader learning goals. Like any powerful learning experience, simulations need to be complemented by meaningful ways to demonstrate and assess understanding. This brings us to our next learning environment: Testing, Performance, and Teaching. Through these varied forms of assessment and demonstration, students discover multiple pathways for showing what they know and further deepening their learning. As we'll explore in the next chapter, when assessment becomes a learning environment rather than just a measurement tool, it creates powerful opportunities for both evaluating and extending student growth.

Let's Take a Deeper Look – Chapter 13

These questions aren't just for pondering – they're invitations to connect these ideas with your own journey and vision as an educator. Take time to explore them deeply, perhaps journaling your thoughts or discussing them with fellow mentors.

1. Consider the "Know, Feel, Do" framework discussed in the chapter. How might you apply this to a simulation in your field of expertise? Provide specific examples for each aspect of the framework.

2. The chapter outlines various forms simulations can take (e.g., historical reenactments, future scenario planning). Which form do you think would be most effective for your scholars, and why?

3. The chapter emphasizes the crucial role of debriefing in the simulation process. Design three specific questions you would ask during a debrief session to encourage reflection, analytical discussion, and real-life connections.

4. The chapter mentions that simulations provide a safe learning environment for risk-taking and experimentation. How would you create this "safe space" while still maintaining the challenge and realism of the simulation?

Resources for Deeper Learning:

> **Simulations Book** by Tatiana Fallon, a step by step workbook to help you create your own simulations as well as a resource for over 45 simulation ideas.[1]
> Available on LEMIHomeschool.com
>
> **LEMI Mentor Training** - a three day immersive program where participants are trained in project-based learning, Leadership Education and the Learning Environments. For more information go to LEMIHomeschool.com

CHAPTER 14

Testing, Performance, and Teaching

Jacob stared at the rows of identical desks, each precisely spaced for test-taking. His stomach churned as he pulled out his #2 pencil and waited for the multiple-choice exam to be distributed. The proctor's voice cut through the silence: "You have sixty minutes. Keep your eyes on your own paper. Begin." Jacob felt his mind going blank, his weeks of memorization slipping away under pressure.

Across town, Emma sat with her small study group, preparing to teach her peers about the American Revolution. She had spent weeks exploring primary sources, crafting engaging activities, and developing ways to help others understand the complex factors that led to independence. Rather than facing multiple-choice questions, she would demonstrate her understanding through teaching, engaging her peers in meaningful discussion, and responding to their questions. Emma felt both challenged and excited—this wasn't just about recalling facts but about synthesizing knowledge and sharing it effectively with others.

These contrasting scenes illustrate two fundamentally different approaches to demonstrating learning. The traditional "conveyor belt" model of education[1] treats testing as a standardized measurement tool, emphasizing memorization and uniform answers. Leadership Education, however, views testing, performance, and teaching as powerful learning environments in themselves. Assessment becomes an opportunity for growth and self-discovery, while performance and teaching provide authentic contexts for demonstrating and deepening understanding.

Understanding the Three Components

The Testing, Performance, and Teaching environment encompasses three distinct but interconnected approaches to demonstrating and deepening learning. Testing provides structured opportunities for students to demonstrate understanding. There are various forms of assessment, from traditional examinations to innovative project-based evaluations. This component includes both formative assessments that guide ongoing learning and summative assessments that measure achievement. Through tools like oral examinations, essay examinations, portfolio development, and self-assessment, testing becomes a pathway for self-discovery rather than merely measuring knowledge.

Performance adds a dynamic dimension to learning demonstration, allowing students to showcase their understanding through active engagement and creative expression. Whether through theatrical productions, musical presentations, public speaking engagements, debate competitions, project demonstrations, or athletic achievements, performance provides authentic contexts for applying knowledge and developing confidence. These opportunities challenge students to synthesize their learning in ways that engage and impact others while building essential leadership and communication skills.

Teaching represents another inspiring component, as it requires students to deepen their own understanding to share knowledge with others effectively. Whether it is through activities like peer tutoring, class presentations, workshop facilitation, mentoring younger students, or community education projects, students discover that teaching others often leads to their own breakthrough moments of understanding. Natural teaching stems from the spontaneous teaching of friends or siblings or having a YouTube channel, and teaching others facilitates exponential growth and learning. This component naturally encourages students to organize their thoughts clearly, anticipate questions, and develop the ability to explain complex ideas in accessible ways. The process of preparing to teach often reveals gaps in understanding that might otherwise go unnoticed, driving students toward deeper mastery of their subject matter. And teaching spontaneously because the student wants to help someone or because they are passionate about something brings deeper understanding and cements knowledge.

Together, these three components create a comprehensive approach to an essential learning environment that develops both competence and character. Each component offers unique benefits while complementing the others, providing multiple pathways for students to show what they know and discover what they still need to learn. This multifaceted approach ensures that students have various opportunities to demonstrate their understanding while developing crucial skills for future leadership and lifelong learning.

Leadership Education vs. Traditional Testing

The Leadership Education approach to testing, performance, and teaching fundamentally differs from traditional "conveyor belt" assessment methods in both philosophy and practice. While conventional education often relies heavily on standardized tests and uniform metrics, Leadership Education views assessment as an active learning environment that promotes growth and discovery.

Traditional "Conveyor Belt" Assessment:

- Emphasizes standardized testing
- Focuses on memorization and recall
- Values uniform answers
- Creates high-pressure testing environments
- Measures against standardized benchmarks
- Often leads to teaching to the test
- Typically offers limited feedback

Leadership Education Assessment approaches demonstration of learning through:

Interactive Methods:

- Group discussions and debates
- Socratic questioning sessions
- Peer review and feedback
- Collaborative problem-solving

- Real-time demonstration of skills
- Active engagement with material

Project-Based Assessment:

- Long-term research projects
- Community service initiatives
- Creative productions
- Portfolio development
- Practical application of knowledge
- Integration across subjects

Authentic Demonstration:

- Real-world problem solving
- Public presentations
- Teaching opportunities
- Performance showcases
- Service learning
- Leadership experiences

The transformation to a more dynamic assessment approach yields significant benefits for student learning and development. By offering multiple pathways to demonstrate knowledge, this method reduces test anxiety while promoting deeper understanding rather than surface-level memorization. Students develop practical skills alongside content knowledge, applying their learning in meaningful contexts. This approach builds confidence through authentic achievement, cultivates leadership capabilities, and instills habits that support lifelong learning.

By reimagining assessment as an active learning environment rather than just a measurement tool, Leadership Education creates opportunities for students to demonstrate their understanding while continuing to grow and develop. This approach recognizes that true learning cannot be fully captured through traditional testing methods alone, and that the process of demonstrating knowledge should itself be a meaningful learning experience.

By reimagining assessment as an active learning environment rather than just a measurement tool, Leadership Education creates opportunities for students to demonstrate their understanding while continuing to grow and develop. This approach recognizes that true learning cannot be fully captured through traditional testing methods alone, and that the process of demonstrating knowledge should itself be a meaningful learning experience.

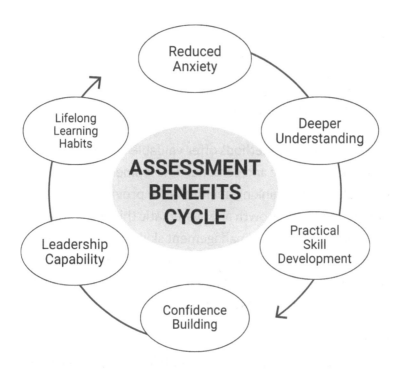

Reduced Anxiety

Deeper Understanding

Practical Skill Development

Confidence Building

Leadership Capability

Lifelong Learning Habits

ASSESSMENT BENEFITS CYCLE

Types of Assessment and Demonstration

Traditional Assessment Methods engage students in demonstrating their understanding through structured, thoughtful evaluation. For example, a written examination might ask students to analyze historical events from multiple perspectives, or a research paper might require students to connect classical ideas to contemporary challenges.

Assessment Methods include:

- Written examinations emphasizing analysis

- Research papers and projects
- Portfolio submissions
- Performance evaluations
- Oral examinations
- Project-based assessments
- Self-reflective assignments

These assessment methods offer valuable benefits to students' academic and personal development. They cultivate critical thinking abilities while providing structured opportunities for growth and systematic thinking. Students develop essential time management skills through these methods, and their progress becomes clearly visible over time, allowing them to track their development and adjust their learning strategies accordingly.

Performance Opportunities create dynamic contexts for students to demonstrate mastery while developing crucial leadership and communication skills. These experiences challenge students to synthesize their learning in ways that engage and impact others.

Performance Opportunities include:

- Shakespeare productions
- Musical recitals
- Speech competitions
- Athletic events
- Art exhibitions
- Debate tournaments
- Scientific demonstrations
- Community presentations

These assessment methods offer valuable benefits to students' academic and personal development. They cultivate critical thinking abilities while providing structured opportunities for growth and systematic thinking. Students develop essential time management skills through these methods, and their progress becomes clearly visible over time, allowing them to track their development and adjust their learning strategies accordingly.

Teaching Contexts provide opportunities for demonstrating and deepening understanding. When students help others grasp complex concepts, they naturally strengthen their own comprehension while developing crucial communication skills.

Teaching Contexts include:

- Peer tutoring programs
- Student-led workshops
- Community education initiatives
- Cross-age mentoring
- Class presentations
- Study group leadership
- Skills demonstration
- Project team leadership

Teaching opportunities benefit students by deepening their subject understanding and developing clear communication skills. The experience builds leadership capabilities while fostering empathy and creating meaningful connections with others. Through teaching, students transform from passive learners into active guides for their peers' understanding.

Through thoughtful integration of these assessment and demonstration methods, Leadership Education creates multiple pathways for students to show what they know while continuing to grow and develop.

Deep Dive: Oral Examinations in Leadership Education

Oral examinations hold a unique place in Leadership Education. They offer dynamic opportunities for students to articulate understanding, think on their feet, and demonstrate mastery through direct interaction. Unlike written tests, oral exams create a real-time dialogue between examiner and student, allowing for immediate clarification, deeper exploration of ideas, and authentic demonstration of understanding.

Structure and Implementation

Oral exams take several forms:

- Individual examinations with a mentor
- Panel discussions with multiple examiners
- Peer-group sessions with collaborative elements
- Public presentations with Q&A components
- Defense of research or projects

Each format can be conducted both informally during regular class discussions and formally as part of end-of-course assessments.

Types of Questions

Effective oral exams employ three distinct question types:

Rapid Fire Questions test foundational knowledge and quick recall. These straightforward questions establish a basic understanding and build confidence early in the examination. Example: "Name three key events leading to the American Revolution."

Conjecture Questions explore deeper thinking and analytical abilities. These open-ended questions invite students to make connections and defend positions. Example: "How might the American Revolution have unfolded differently if France hadn't provided support?"

Comprehension Questions assess understanding of complex concepts and principles. These questions require students to explain ideas clearly and demonstrate genuine mastery. Example: "Explain how the principle of representation without taxation influenced colonial thinking, and connect it to modern political debates."

Benefits of Oral Examination

This assessment method uniquely develops:

- Verbal communication skills
- Quick analytical thinking
- Confidence in articulating ideas
- Professional poise under pressure
- Ability to engage in intellectual discourse
- Skill in defending positions respectfully

- Capacity to make real-time connections
- Comfort with academic dialogue

Mentor Guidance

Mentors support successful oral examinations by:

- Providing clear expectations beforehand
- Creating a supportive examination environment
- Asking progressively challenging questions
- Offering encouraging non-verbal feedback
- Following up on incomplete answers
- Allowing appropriate thinking time
- Guiding students toward deeper insights
- Closing with constructive feedback

Through thoughtful implementation of oral examinations, mentors help students develop not just subject mastery but also crucial communication and leadership skills that serve them well beyond their academic careers. The confidence and capability built through these experiences prepare students for future professional and academic challenges where articulate expression of ideas is essential.

Implementation Guidelines

The effective implementation of testing, performance, and teaching as learning environments requires careful attention to physical space, emotional safety, and developmental readiness. Here's how to create optimal conditions across each component.

Creating Supportive Settings

For effective implementation, careful attention must be paid to both physical and emotional elements of this learning environment. The physical space should feature flexible seating arrangements, dedicated performance areas, and comfortable teaching spaces with proper lighting and ventilation. External distractions should be minimized, while necessary resources remain readily accessible. Proper acoustics for oral presentations and options for both individual and group work are essential.

Equally important is creating emotional safety. This requires establishing clear expectations upfront and fostering supportive peer environments where effort and growth are celebrated. Mistakes should be framed as learning opportunities, with adequate preparation time provided. Private feedback spaces allow for personal reflection and guidance, while progressive challenges help build confidence. Throughout, consistent and fair standards must be maintained to support student development.

Implementation Across Learning Phases

Discovery Phase (Ages 0-11):

Assessment at this level should emphasize discovery and joy in learning. In the younger ages, these assessments are instigated by the child. A child will often announce, to any who are listening, their thoughts and stream of consciousness about the world around them.

As the child grows, a simple show and tell when students are old enough provides an excellent example of integrated assessment, performance, and teaching:

- Students select and research something meaningful to them
- They prepare a short presentation for their family, friends, or classmates
- They answer questions from peers and teachers
- They practice public speaking in a supportive environment
- They learn to give and receive positive feedback
- They develop confidence in sharing knowledge
- They experience the joy of teaching others
- They build presentation skills naturally

Practice Scholar (Ages 12-14):

The Harvest Dinner Project in LEMI's Georgics Project demonstrates how students can begin taking on more scholarly responsibilities through a comprehensive experiential learning approach. Students start by researching the history and cultivation of their chosen food, delving into its agricultural background and cultural significance. As part of the project, they prepare a dish to share with the community and present their findings at a formal dinner, where they must field questions about their research. Through this process, students learn to make meaningful connections between ancient agricultural principles and modern food production methods. The project helps them develop formal presentation skills as they share their knowledge with others. Perhaps most importantly, students experience the deep satisfaction of feeding others while developing a genuine appreciation for the origins of everyday items. This hands-on project exemplifies how Practice Scholars can engage with academic content in ways that build both practical skills and scholarly understanding.

Apprentice Scholar (Ages 14-16):

LEMI's Classical Acting project exemplifies the increasing complexity and leadership opportunities available to Apprentice Scholars. In this comprehensive theatrical endeavor, students take on significant leadership roles in production planning while conducting research into historical context and dramatic interpretation. They develop their directorial abilities by leading scenes and coaching fellow actors, while simultaneously managing both artistic and logistical aspects of the production. Throughout the process, students work collaboratively to solve various challenges that arise. They learn to thoughtfully adapt Shakespeare's language for modern audiences while maintaining the integrity of the original work. The project also involves creating promotional materials and programs, giving students experience with the marketing aspects of theater. Through this immersive experience, students gain a thorough understanding of the full cycle of theatrical production, from initial planning through final performance.

Self-Directed Scholar (Ages 16-18):

LEMI's Edison Project's mastermind groups demonstrate an integration of testing, performance, and teaching approaches for Self-Directed Scholars. Students begin by designing and pursuing individual research projects, while regularly presenting progress updates to their peers to maintain accountability and momentum. Throughout the process, they engage in a dynamic exchange of constructive feedback, both providing and receiving insights that help refine their work. Students demonstrate flexibility and responsiveness by adjusting their projects based on peer input, while continuously developing their professional presentation skills. The project structure helps them build robust project management capabilities as they navigate complex, long-term research endeavors. Students learn to clearly articulate both challenges and solutions, developing crucial communication skills for leadership. Through this collaborative approach, they experience authentic peer mentoring, creating a supportive learning community that enhances everyone's growth and development.

Each of these examples shows how testing, performance, and teaching naturally integrate to create meaningful learning experiences appropriate to students' developmental levels. Through these carefully designed projects, students progressively develop both competence and confidence in demonstrating and sharing their learning.

Practical Tips for Success

Preparation:
- Provide clear assessment criteria
- Allow adequate preparation time
- Offer necessary resources
- Give specific feedback for improvement
- Create practice opportunities

- Share exemplary examples
- Establish clear timelines
- Build progressive challenges

Support During Events:

- Maintain encouraging presence
- Provide necessary guidance
- Monitor student well-being
- Address concerns promptly
- Document progress
- Celebrate effort
- Offer technical support
- Enable peer support

Follow-Through:

- Conduct thorough debriefing
- Document learning outcomes
- Plan next steps
- Share successes
- Address challenges
- Adjust future approaches
- Build on achievements
- Connect to broader goals

Keys to Success

Remember these fundamental principles:

- Match challenges to student readiness
- Build confidence through progressive success
- Maintain high standards with appropriate support
- Create opportunities for meaningful practice
- Celebrate growth and effort
- Document progress systematically
- Adjust approaches based on feedback

- Keep focus on learning rather than performance

Through thoughtful implementation of these guidelines, mentors can create powerful learning experiences that develop both competence and character. The key lies in maintaining flexibility while providing appropriate structure and support for each student's growth journey.

Embracing Growth Through Innovative Assessment

The Testing, Performance, and Teaching environment in Leadership Education represents a paradigm shift from traditional assessment methods. By reimagining testing as a tool for learning and self-discovery, this approach creates powerful opportunities for students to demonstrate their understanding while simultaneously deepening their knowledge and developing crucial skills.

Through the integration of assessment methods, performance opportunities, and teaching opportunities, students engage in a multifaceted process of growth and development. This comprehensive approach not only evaluates learning but also fosters critical thinking, communication skills, and leadership capabilities.

However, even the most powerful assessment experiences benefit from structured reflection and processing. This brings us to our next learning environment: Debriefing. Through thoughtful debriefing, students transform their testing, performance, and teaching experiences into lasting insights and practical wisdom. As we'll explore in the next chapter, the art of debriefing helps students extract maximum value from every learning opportunity, turning moments of assessment into springboards for deeper understanding and continued growth.

Let's Take a Deeper Look — Chapter 14

These questions aren't just for pondering – they're invitations to connect these ideas with your own journey and vision as an educator. Take time to explore them deeply, perhaps journaling your thoughts or discussing them with fellow mentors.

1. Think about your own experiences with traditional testing versus more dynamic forms of assessment like performance and teaching. How did these different approaches affect your learning and retention? How might these experiences inform your approach to assessing students?

2. The chapter describes assessment as an active learning environment rather than just a measurement tool. What specific changes would you need to make in your current practice to fully embrace this perspective? What challenges might you face in implementing these changes?

3. Consider the three components of assessment discussed (testing, performance, and teaching). How do these work together to provide a more complete picture of student understanding? Can you think of a specific topic or project where you could implement all three approaches?

4. This chapter emphasizes that traditional testing

methods can be reimagined to promote deeper learning. Choose a standard test or quiz you currently use. How could you modify it to become more of a learning experience while still effectively measuring understanding?

5. Reflect on the Leadership Education approach to assessment versus traditional "conveyor belt" methods. What mindset shifts would be necessary – for both educators and students – to successfully implement this more dynamic approach to assessment? How might you facilitate these shifts in your educational setting?

Resources for Deeper Learning:

> **LEMI Mentor Training** - a three day immersive program where participants are trained in project-based learning, Leadership Education and the Learning Environments. For more information go to LEMIHomeschool.com

CHAPTER 15

Debriefing:
Transforming Experience
into Understanding

Sarah watched her students slowly emerge from their roles in the LEMI Georgics Project (a Practice Scholar project) post-disaster simulation, their faces reflecting intense emotions. Michael, representing Deweyville's doctor, had passionately argued for prioritizing medical supplies, while Emma, typically reserved, found her voice as Southtown's agricultural expert, challenging others about food sustainability. When discussions about sharing limited resources grew heated, Sarah called for a brief pause to let tensions settle.

Now, as the two communities' survival plans lay before them, Sarah faced a crucial moment. Her students hadn't just planned for survival—they had simulated making difficult choices about resources, leadership, and community cooperation. Some sat in thoughtful silence, while others buzzed with energy, eager to share their experiences. Without thoughtful debriefing, even this powerful simulation might remain just an exciting memory rather than a transformative lesson about leadership, resource management, and human nature in times of crisis.

The next thirty minutes would determine whether students could connect their emotional experience to deeper insights about leadership and community resilience. As Sarah gathered them into a circle, she knew that the skill with which she guided their reflection would make all the difference.

Throughout our exploration of effective mentorship and learning, we've emphasized the importance of active engagement, critical thinking, compassion, and emotional intelligence. Now, we turn our attention to a crucial component that ties these elements together and solidifies learning: the debrief.

Debriefing is not merely a conclusion to a learning activity; it is a powerful tool for processing experiences, extracting meaningful insights, and bridging the gap between theory and practice. In this chapter, we'll explore this transformational experience and how it can be used to enhance various learning environments, from simulations to lectures and discussions.

Understanding Debriefing

At its core, debriefing is a structured reflection process that transforms experiences into lasting insights. Like a bridge between experience and understanding, effective debriefing helps students process what happened, analyze why it matters, and determine how to apply their learning.

Core Elements

1. **Emotional Processing:** Students need opportunities to acknowledge and process their emotional responses

before they can engage in deeper analysis. Whether excited, frustrated, or uncertain, these feelings contain valuable information about the learning experience.

2. **Cognitive Integration:** Through guided reflection, students connect their experience to existing knowledge and discover new insights. This might involve recognizing patterns, questioning assumptions, or making unexpected connections between ideas.

3. **Practical Application:** Effective debriefing helps students identify specific ways to apply their learning to real situations. This transforms abstract understanding into actionable insights.

The "Know, Feel, Do" Framework

This simple but powerful framework guides the debriefing process:

Know: What did we learn?
- Key insights gained about self, others, human nature, and the scenario
- Principles discovered
- Patterns recognized
- Questions raised

Feel: How did we experience it?
- Emotional reactions
- Challenging moments
- Breakthrough insights
- Group dynamics

Do: How will we use it?
- Practical applications
- Behavior changes

Debriefing: Transforming Experience into Understanding

- New approaches to try
- Next steps for growth

Types of Debriefing Sessions

1. Quick Debrief (5-10 minutes) Ideal for:

   - Wrapping up class discussions
   - Processing short activities
   - Assessing an assignment with the following questions:
     - What did you do well?
     - What would you improve for next time?
   - Checking understanding key questions:
     - What stood out?
     - What surprised you?
     - What will you take away?

2. Standard Debrief (15-30 minutes) Suited for:

   - Most simulations
   - Complex discussions
   - Project completion focus areas:
     - Experience processing
     - Pattern recognition
     - Application planning

3. Extended Debrief (45-60 minutes) Essential for:

   - Major simulations
   - Intense emotional experiences
   - Significant project conclusions

Each type serves specific purposes, and skilled mentors

learn to match the debriefing format to the learning experience and available time. The key is maintaining focus on transforming experience into meaningful learning through structured reflection.

Debriefing Across Learning Phases

Discovery Level (Ages 0-11)

Keep debriefing playful and concrete when the student is old enough for debriefs. For the little ones, ages 0-3, it is usually just enough to role-play and practice behavior without a debrief. Use simple questions that help students connect experiences to tangible learning:

- "What was your favorite part?"
- "What surprised you?"
- "How would you feel if that happened to you?"
- "What would you do differently next time?" Incorporate movement and drawing to help process experiences. Keep sessions brief (5-10 minutes) and maintain high engagement through variety.

Practice Scholar (Ages 12-14)

Begin introducing more structured reflection while maintaining active engagement:

- Use round-robin sharing to ensure all voices are heard
- Introduce basic analysis through comparison questions
- Help students identify patterns in their experience
- Guide them in making connections to other learning sessions, which can extend to 15-20 minutes, balancing discussion with activity.

Apprentice Scholar (Ages 14-16)

Deepen analytical thinking while developing leadership skills:

- Encourage students to lead portions of the debrief
- Ask more complex "why" and "how" questions
- Guide connections between experience and principles
- Help students identify applications to other situations. Sessions typically run 20-30 minutes, with greater emphasis on discussion and insight.
- Debriefing can include journaling, sharing with their classmate, and discussion.

Self-Directed Scholar (Ages 16-18)

Foster meaningful reflection and application:

- Students may help facilitate debriefing sessions
- Explore systemic implications and broader principles
- Develop action plans based on insights
- Connect learning to leadership and life goals Sessions can extend to 45-60 minutes, incorporating individual reflection, small group discussion, and collective synthesis.

Remember: These guidelines should flex based on group dynamics and individual readiness. The goal is to match the depth and structure of debriefing to students' developmental capabilities while consistently pushing toward deeper understanding.

The Mentor's Role

1. **Setting the Tone:** Creating a safe space for honest

sharing is the foundation of effective debriefing. The mentor must model openness and vulnerability while establishing clear guidelines for respectful dialogue. Body language and physical presence matter significantly; use welcoming gestures and position yourself as part of the circle, not above it. This inclusive atmosphere encourages authentic participation and deeper reflection.

2. **Asking Powerful Questions**: Begin with broad observation questions like "What happened?" before moving to emotional processing with "How did you feel?" Progress to analysis through "Why do you think that occurred?" Then guide connections to leadership principles, and finally focus on action with "How will you apply this?" This progressive questioning helps students move from surface observations to meaningful insights.

3. **Managing Group Dynamics:** Successful debriefing requires skillful management of group participation. Draw out quieter voices while gently redirecting dominant speakers. Address conflicts constructively, viewing them as opportunities for learning. When needed, break into smaller groups to encourage more intimate sharing and ensure all voices are heard.

4. **Reading the Room:** Stay attuned to body language indicating engagement or resistance, emotional reactions requiring attention, and signs of confusion or breakthrough. Monitor energy levels and attention spans while watching for moments when the group is ready to push deeper. This awareness allows you to adjust your approach in real time to maintain productive discussion.

5. **Synthesizing Insights:** Help students recognize patterns and connections between individual comments and

broader themes. Guide the group in constructing meaning together while documenting key insights for future reference. Bridge different perspectives to create a richer understanding of the experience and its implications.

6. **Connecting to Action:** Transform insights into concrete steps by guiding practical application planning. Help students identify specific actions they'll take and create accountability structures to support implementation. Schedule follow-up discussions to reinforce learning and support ongoing application of insights.

Remember: Your role is to facilitate discovery. The most powerful insights often emerge when students make their own connections within a well-structured reflection process.

Practical Implementation

Creating Effective Debriefs

Start with a clear structure while remaining flexible enough to follow meaningful tangents. Plan your timing intentionally: opening reflection (20%), main discussion (60%), and action planning (20%). Consider your physical space – arrange seating in a circle when possible to encourage equal participation. Keep essential materials like reflection journals, whiteboard, or documentation tools easily accessible.

Common Challenges and Solutions

1. Surface-Level Responses – When students offer superficial comments like "It was fun" or "I liked it,"

probe deeper with follow-up questions. Ask for specific examples or moments that led to those feelings. Share brief examples of deeper reflection to model the expected level of analysis. Sometimes offering think-time before sharing helps students formulate more thoughtful responses.

2. Emotional Intensity – Strong emotional responses, whether from heated debates or powerful realizations, require careful handling. Acknowledge feelings without judgment. Create space for processing through individual journaling or paired discussions before opening to the full group. Maintain professional boundaries while showing empathy, and know when to refer students for additional support.

3. Uneven Participation – Address dominating voices by implementing structured sharing methods like round-robin responses. Create opportunities for written reflection before discussion so quieter students can prepare their thoughts. Use small group breakouts to build confidence before full group sharing. When needed, have private conversations with particularly dominant or reluctant participants.

4. Time Management – Start and end on time to demonstrate respect for everyone's schedule. Use a timer for different segments of the debrief. When time runs short, prioritize essential questions and consolidate similar themes. Keep a flexible outline that identifies core discussion points while leaving room for unexpected insights.

Adapting to Different Learning Environments

For Simulations: Focus initial questions on emerging from character roles before moving to analysis. Address both individual experiences and group dynamics. Help students connect historical or fictional scenarios to contemporary applications.

For Discussions: Emphasize capturing key insights and unresolved questions. Guide students in recognizing how their thinking evolved through the conversation. Identify practical applications of theoretical concepts.

For Projects: Focus on process as well as outcomes. Explore what worked, what didn't, and why. Help students articulate lessons learned and implications for future work.

Assessment and Refinement

Document key themes and insights emerging from each debrief. Note which questions sparked the richest discussion and which fell flat. Pay attention to group dynamics and energy patterns. Use this information to refine your approach over time, building a repertoire of effective strategies for different situations.

Remember: Effective debriefing improves with practice. Start with these foundational elements and gradually incorporate more techniques as you gain experience and confidence in facilitating reflection.

From Experience to Insight: The Power of Strategic Debriefing

In our opening scene, Sarah's students had just experienced

the emotional intensity of the LEMI Georgics Project post-disaster simulation. Through skillful debriefing, those powerful feelings and experiences about survival, resource management, and community cooperation transformed into lasting insights about leadership, human nature, and the challenges of building consensus during crisis. This transformation – from raw experience to meaningful understanding – represents the heart of effective debriefing.

The tools we've explored – structured reflection, powerful questioning, and thoughtful facilitation – work together to create lasting learning. Whether processing a heated debate, unpacking a complex simulation, or reflecting on individual discoveries, strategic debriefing helps students connect experiences to future actions.

As mentors, we create the conditions where genuine insights emerge. Through attention to emotional safety, balanced participation, and progressive reflection, we help students develop both the skills and the habit of transforming experience into understanding. These capabilities serve them not just in the classroom but throughout their lives as leaders and learners.

Remember that mastering debriefing is itself a journey of continuous learning. Each session offers opportunities to refine our skills and deepen our understanding of how people learn through reflection. As you incorporate these principles into your mentoring, trust that every thoughtfully facilitated debrief moves your students closer to becoming the kind of reflective, insightful leaders our world needs.

As we move to our final chapter, we'll explore how these ten learning environments work together to create educational experiences that develop both character and capability in tomorrow's leaders.

Let's Take a Deeper Look – Chapter 15

These questions aren't just for pondering – they're invitations to connect these ideas with your own journey and vision as an educator. Take time to explore them deeply, perhaps journaling your thoughts or discussing them with fellow mentors.

1. Think about a recent learning experience you facilitated. How might incorporating a structured debrief have enhanced the learning outcomes? What specific elements would you include in this debrief?

2. How might you apply the "Know, Feel, Do" framework to a debrief in your educational setting? Provide an example of a question you might ask for each aspect of the framework.

3. Reflect on a time when you participated in or led a particularly effective debrief. What made it successful? How can you incorporate those elements into your future debriefing practices?

4. The role of the mentor in debriefing is described as "crucial but delicate." How do you balance guiding the process without dominating it? Provide specific examples from your experience or ideas you'd like to try.

5. The chapter emphasizes the importance of open-ended questions in debriefing. Create three open-ended questions you might use to stimulate deep reflection in a debrief related to your field.

Resources for Deeper Learning:

The Mentor's Handbook by Aneladee Milne. Available at LEMIHomeschool.com[1]

CHAPTER 16

Making It Work: A Practical Guide to Implementing Learning Environments

Leah reviewed her lesson plans for tomorrow's American Revolution unit, each component carefully chosen. She would begin with Thomas Paine's "Common Sense,"[1] using its passionate call for independence to spark discussion. A simulation of the Boston Tea Party would transform abstract concepts into an experience to be lived and felt. Through guided reading and tutorials, students would develop their own understanding, eventually teaching younger students about colonial life.

Leah smiled, remembering her early days of teaching when she relied solely on lectures and textbooks. Now she understood that true learning emerged from the thoughtful orchestration of different environments, each one building upon and enhancing the others.

Like Leah's carefully crafted lesson plan, effective Leadership Education requires skillful integration of multiple learning environments. Throughout this book, we've explored each environment in detail—from Example to Debriefing. Now it's time to examine how these environments work together to create transformative learning experiences.

This integration happens naturally in LEMI Scholar Projects, where each environment serves a specific purpose while contributing to a greater whole. Let's look at how these environments combine to create powerful learning experiences that develop both competence and character.

In Scholar Projects

Each of the LEMI Scholar Projects exemplify the integration of these environments. For example:

How Key of Liberty Uses the Learning Environments:
- Example: Historical figure study
- Discussion: Constitutional principles
- Reading: Primary sources
- Writing: Opinion papers
- Tutorial: Research guidance
- Coaching: Presentation skills
- Lecture: Historical context and background
- Simulation: Continental Congress
- Performance: Memorization of the Declaration of Independence
- Debrief: Connecting past to present

Each project combines environments to help students:

- Engage deeply with material
- Develop critical thinking
- Build leadership capabilities
- Progress through Leadership Ladders
- Create meaningful connections

Whether you have access to the LEMI Scholar Projects or not, this book can help you in your mentoring. Keep reading to see how to get the most out of this book.

How to Use This Book

A. As a Reference Guide

This book provides the framework and tools for creating leadership educational experiences. As you implement these environments:

1. Start where you are.

2. Master one environment at a time.

3. Document what works.

4. Share insights with other mentors.

Keep this book close and use it as a reference guide when learning to implement or enhance any learning environment:

1. Review the relevant chapter for:

- Core principles and best practices
- Phase-specific adaptations
- Common challenges and solutions
- Implementation guidelines

2. Consider integration opportunities when classes haven't incorporated the use of the learning environments:

- Which environments naturally complement your current focus?
- How can you create smooth transitions between environments?
- What combinations will best serve your learning objectives?

A Practical Guide to Implementing Learning Environments

3. Check phase-appropriate applications:

  - Discovery Phase guidelines
  - Practice Scholar adaptations
  - Apprentice Scholar implementations
  - Self-Directed Scholar approaches

Where there is already a blend of these learning environments, use this book to deepen your expertise in each specific environment you employ.

B. For Continuous Improvement

Use this book to:

1. Assess current practices

2. Identify growth opportunities

3. Expand your repertoire

4. Refine implementation

5. Deepen understanding

C. Enhancing Existing Classes

If you're teaching a class that doesn't yet incorporate multiple learning environments and you have the freedom to incorporate them, here are practical ways to expand your approach:

For Literature Classes:

  - Add simulation by having students act out key scenes.
  - Include coaching sessions for writing development.

- Incorporate tutorials for deeper text analysis.
- Add student teaching opportunities through literature circles.

For Science Classes:

- Introduce the science principle through doing experiments (simulation).
- Include coaching for lab technique development.
- Use tutorials for complex concept mastery.
- Implement student-led teaching of basic principles.

For History Classes:

- Create simulations of historical events.
- Use coaching for research skill development.
- Add tutorials for primary source analysis.
- Implement student teaching of timeline events.
- Include debriefing after major units.

For Math Classes:

- Start with clear examples of problem-solving.
- Add tutorials for struggling students.
- Share inspiring stories of mathematicians and scientists to inspire the students.
- Implement peer teaching of mastered concepts.
- Use coaching for advanced problem approaches.
- Include debriefing after complex problem sets.

Consider These Powerful Combinations

In addition to those practical ideas, in classes where they are not already built in as they are in the Scholar Projects, consider these powerful combinations:

Workshop and Discussion

When a mentor models and workshops deep analysis of a text and then guides students in collaborative dialogue, learning becomes both visible and interactive. Students see the principles in action before practicing them themselves, creating a natural progression from observation to engagement.

Reading and Writing

These environments create a dynamic cycle of input and output. Deep reading naturally inspires written reflection, while the act of writing often sends students back to their reading with new questions and insights. Each environment strengthens the other, developing both comprehension and expression.

Simulation and Debrief

Simulations provide rich experiences that come alive through thoughtful debriefing. Without the simulation, the debrief lacks substance; without the debrief, the simulation risks becoming merely an engaging activity rather than a transformative learning experience. Together, they create lasting understanding.

Tutorial and Coaching

While tutorials focus on understanding concepts and

materials, coaching develops specific skills and abilities. When used together, they help students both grasp ideas and implement them effectively. A tutorial might help a student understand the principles of effective writing, while coaching helps them apply these principles to their own work.

Lecture and Testing

When skillfully combined, lectures and testing create a natural cycle of learning and discovery. The lecture sparks curiosity and provides essential context, while testing changes from a source of stress into an opportunity for students to explore and demonstrate their understanding. Through this partnership, students engage with material first as eager listeners, then as active participants in their own learning journey. They discover not just what they know, but also which areas intrigue them enough to warrant deeper investigation. The testing environment becomes a space for both demonstrating mastery and identifying promising paths for further exploration.

Seize the Moment

The real power emerges when we seize the moment that a learning environment creates, allowing the moment to expand as light bulbs and epiphanies emerge in the students.

Choose environments based on what you want your students to know, feel, and do, and on asking how the material can be delivered and engaged with effectively.

Some material lends itself best to specific environments. Difficult but shorter texts can be used as document studies in tutorials. New information and historical context can be delivered well in lecture, yet some historical context can be delivered through simulations. Your job is to do your best to help the students engage with the material in a meaningful way.

A Vision for Leadership Education

You now have a comprehensive framework for creating Leadership Education. These ten learning environments— Example, Discussion, Reading, Writing, Tutorial, Coaching, Lecture, Simulation, Testing/Performance/Teaching, and Debriefing—represent essential tools for developing the leaders our world desperately needs.

Each environment serves a distinct and crucial purpose:

- Example demonstrates what's possible
- Discussion and Reading build critical thinking
- Writing helps students find their voice
- Tutorials and Coaching provide personalized guidance
- Lectures inspire and inform
- Simulations bridge theory and practice
- Testing/Performance/Teaching allows authentic demonstration
- Debriefing transforms experience into wisdom

Understanding these environments is just the beginning— this vision requires action. Start where you are, with the students before you. Master one environment at a time, observing how it works in your unique circumstances. Adapt thoughtfully for different learning phases while maintaining unwavering focus on student growth. And never stop developing your own capacity as a mentor.

Our world faces unprecedented challenges that will require leaders of unusual wisdom, integrity, and capability. The rapid pace of change, increasing complexity of global challenges, and profound questions about humanity's future demand education that goes beyond information transfer to true transformation. Through these learning environments, we help students discover not only knowledge but their capacity for meaningful contribution.

You are not just teaching subjects—you are developing the leaders who will shape tomorrow. In fact, we often remind our mentors that their subject is the student. Every time you thoughtfully implement these environments, you create impact that extends far beyond your classroom. Each student who discovers their voice, develops their thinking, and embraces their potential for leadership becomes a force for positive change in their community and world.

The future of Leadership Education lies in your hands now. These environments provide the foundation for creating experiences that develop capable, thoughtful leaders. Your dedication to this approach, your willingness to grow as a mentor, and your commitment to developing future leaders will influence generations to come.

The world is waiting. Your students are ready. The tools are in your hands.

A Practical Guide to Implementing Learning Environments

What will you create?

How will you help guide the next generation of leaders?

The time to begin is now.

Let's Take a Deeper Look — Chapter 16

These questions aren't just for pondering – they're invitations to connect these ideas with your own journey and vision as an educator. Take time to explore them deeply, perhaps journaling your thoughts or discussing them with fellow mentors.

1. Looking across all ten learning environments discussed in this book, which ones do you currently use most effectively, and which offer the greatest opportunity for growth in your mentoring practice? How might strengthening your use of less familiar environments enhance your overall effectiveness as a mentor?

2. Think about a specific student or group you mentor. How could you create a more harmonious "learning symphony" by thoughtfully combining different environments to serve their unique needs and developmental stage? Consider creating a specific plan that integrates at least three environments to achieve a particular learning objective.

3. This book emphasizes the progression through different phases of learning (Discovery, Practice Scholar, Apprentice Scholar, and Self-Directed Scholar). How might your implementation of the ten learning environments need to shift as students progress through these phases? Provide specific examples of how you would adapt your approach.

4. Throughout this book, we've explored how Leadership Education differs from conventional "conveyor belt" education. Reflecting on your own educational journey and mentoring experience, what key mindset shifts have you needed (or still need) to make to fully embrace and implement the Leadership Education approach? How might these shifts influence your future implementation of the learning environments?

5. The goal of Leadership Education is to develop individuals capable of thoughtful leadership, lifelong learning, and meaningful contribution. Looking back at all ten environments, how do they work together to achieve this goal? Which environments do you think are most crucial for developing these specific capacities in your students right now?

GLOSSARY

ABILITIES – One of the five Leadership Ladders referring to character qualities and capabilities that guide tools and skills; includes traits like resilience, empathy, and integrity.

ADAPTING – The process of modifying learning environments to meet students' developmental stages, needs, and capabilities.

ANALYTICAL READING – The third level of reading involving active, intense engagement with text, including questioning, identifying arguments, and evaluating logic.[1]

ANNOTATION – A systematic approach to documenting thoughts, questions, and insights while reading through marginal notes, highlighting, and other marking systems.

APPRENTICE SCHOLAR – A phase of learning (typically ages 14-16) characterized by increased academic rigor, deeper engagement with classic texts, and development of research and writing skills, with approximately 40 hours of weekly study time.

AUDIENCE – The intended readers for a piece of writing, which influences tone, style, and content choices.

BENT STORIES – Narratives that distort reality by presenting wrong as right or suggesting that truth is entirely relative.[2]

BROKEN STORIES – Works that honestly portray the

brokenness in the world without offering resolution.[3]

CHARACTER DEVELOPMENT – A fundamental focus of the Discovery Phase, involving the cultivation of emotional security, moral compass, and foundational virtues.

COACHING – A learning environment where focused mentorship develops both skill and character.

COACHING CYCLE – The systematic process of attempt, feedback, and refinement that characterizes effective coaching.

COLLABORATIVE LEARNING – A learning approach where students work together to explore ideas and develop understanding through shared discovery and discussion.

COGNITIVE INTEGRATION – The process during debriefing where students connect their experience to existing knowledge and discover new insights.

COLLOQUIA – Formal, structured discussion sessions typically lasting 1-2 hours, involving 6 to 30 participants centered on classic texts or significant works that participants have studied in advance.

CONSTRUCTIVE FEEDBACK – Specific, actionable guidance provided to help students improve their performance or understanding.

CONTENT – The educational material, including classics, primary sources, life experiences, and other learning resources that students engage with during their educational journey.

CONVEYOR BELT EDUCATION – A traditional educational approach focused on standardized instruction and predetermined outcomes, contrasting with Leadership Education's personalized approach.[4]

CRISIS MANAGEMENT EXERCISES – Simulations that place students under pressure to handle emergency situations, teaching rapid decision-making and team coordination.

DEBRIEF – A learning environment where experience crystallizes into "ahas" and lasting wisdom.

DISCOVERY PHASE – The foundational learning phase (ages 0-11) that weaves together natural curiosity and character development, focusing on wonder, exploration, and establishing strong emotional security.

DOCUMENT STUDY – A focused examination of primary sources and significant texts that provides a framework for developing critical reading and analytical skills.

EDUCABLE – A state of being where one is able to be educated. The student's role is to be educable.

EDUCERE – The Latin root meaning "to lead out" or "draw out," which forms the philosophical foundation of Leadership Education's approach.[5]

ELEMENTARY READING – The first level of reading

involving basic decoding and recognition of words and simple sentences.[6]

EMOTIONAL BOUNDARIES – Defined limits that ensure psychological safety during simulations while allowing for challenging experiences.

EMOTIONAL INTELLIGENCE – The ability to recognize, understand, and manage one's own emotions while effectively responding to the emotions of others; a key component demonstrated through example.

EMOTIONAL PROCESSING – The initial phase of debriefing where students acknowledge and process their emotional responses to an experience.

ENGAGEMENT – Active participation and investment in the learning process, characterized by curiosity, attention, and meaningful interaction with content and others.

ETHOS – The element of credibility and trustworthiness in presentation, one of the five classical rhetorical elements.[7]

EXAMPLE – A learning environment where principles come alive through actions rather than just words.

FLOW – One of the six points of editing concerning smooth transitions and logical progression of ideas in writing.

FORMAL LECTURES – Structured presentations delivered from a written text by subject matter experts, with questions typically reserved for the end.

FORMS – Ways of doing and being – specific patterns of action, behavior, or thought that consistently lead to particular results, often explored through discussion of classic texts.

FUTURISTIC SCENARIO PLANNING – Simulations that challenge students to apply problem-solving skills in unfamiliar contexts.

GROUP DISCUSSION – A more informal, flexible environment where students explore ideas, solve problems, and build confidence in sharing their thoughts.

GROUP DISCUSSION/COLLOQUIA – A learning environment where ideas spark and grow through shared exploration.

GROWTH MINDSET – The belief that abilities and skills can be developed through dedication, hard work, and continuous learning.[8]

HEALING STORIES – Narratives that acknowledge brokenness but offer hope and the possibility of redemption.[9]

HISTORICAL REENACTMENTS – Simulations that transport students into pivotal moments of history for firsthand experience.

INCREMENTAL PROGRESS – The gradual development of skills and abilities through systematic practice and coaching.

INFORMAL LECTURES – Presentations following an outline format that welcome interaction throughout the delivery.

INSPECTIONAL READING – The second level of reading involving basic comprehension and the ability to grasp main ideas and summarize content.[10]

INTELLECTUAL RISK-TAKING – The willingness to share incomplete ideas and explore uncertain territory in pursuit of deeper understanding during tutorials.

INTERACTIVE PRESENTATION – A lecture style that incorporates audience participation and engagement.

ITERATIVE LEARNING – A process where students repeatedly practice and refine skills based on coaching feedback.

KNOW, FEEL, DO – A framework for setting clear learning objectives: what students should understand (know), experience emotionally (feel), and be able to accomplish (do).

KNOWLEDGE – One of the five Leadership Ladders representing the foundational understanding and information needed to support learning and growth.

LEADERSHIP EDUCATION – An educational approach that draws from the Latin root "educere" meaning "to lead out" or "draw out," recognizing that each person carries unique potential waiting to unfold. It is based on the student's agency and the mentor's invitation to reach one's potential through focused attention and purpose driven work.

LEADERSHIP EDUCATIONAL TEAM – The collective group of key players in Leadership Education: The Student, Mentors and Teachers, Parents, Educational Content, Peers, and Learning Environments.

LEADERSHIP LADDERS (V-MASK) – A framework of five integrated components (Vision, Mission, Abilities, Skills, and Knowledge) that help mentors identify and address student roadblocks to growth.

LEARNING ENVIRONMENTS – Specifically crafted experiences that facilitate and shape how students connect with ideas, build skills, and grow into their potential; not just physical spaces, but approaches to learning.

LEARNING ZONE – The optimal state where genuine learning, change, and growth occur naturally through the effective interaction of all key players in the educational process.

LECTURE – A learning environment where inspiration meets information.

LEXIS – The element of language choice and usage in presentation, one of the five classical rhetorical elements.[11]

LIBER COMMUNITIES – Groups where families come together to offer Leadership Education through collaborative efforts, creating spaces where deep relationships and education flourish.

LOGOS – The element of logic and reasoning in presentation, one of the five classical rhetorical elements.

MENTORS – Guides who focus primarily on the growth and development of the student, helping them navigate challenges and discover their potential.

MICRO SCHOOLS – Educational settings where small class sizes enable truly personalized attention while maintaining flexibility to partner with other families for specialized learning opportunities.

MISSION – One of the five Leadership Ladders representing a student's understanding of their unique purpose and potential contribution to the world.

NATURAL CURIOSITY – A key component of the Discovery Phase where children naturally explore and engage with their world, leading to organic learning and development.

PARENT MENTOR – A parent who takes an active role in their child's education, providing guidance, support, and maintaining regular communication about educational and personal progress.

PATHOS – The element of emotional connection and passion in presentation, one of the five classical rhetorical elements.[12]

PEERS – Fellow students who contribute to the learning environment through collaboration, discussion, and shared growth experiences.

PHASES OF LEARNING – The distinct developmental stages through which students progress in Leadership Education: Discovery Phase, Scholar Phase (including Practice Scholar, Apprentice Scholar, and Self-Directed Scholar), Depth Phase, and Mission Phase.

PHYSICAL BOUNDARIES – Clearly defined spatial limits for simulation activities that ensure safety and appropriate engagement.

PHYSICAL CHALLENGES – Tangible problems requiring teamwork, strategy, and creative thinking to solve.

PRACTICE SCHOLAR – The initial Scholar Phase (typically ages 12-14) where students begin developing scholarly habits and engage in 15-25 hours of weekly discretionary study time.

READABILITY – One of the six points of editing focusing on visual presentation and accessibility of the text.

READING – A learning environment where minds expand and perspectives shift through encounters with powerful ideas.

ROADBLOCK – An obstacle to student growth that can be identified and addressed through the Leadership Ladders framework.

ROLE-PLAYING EXERCISES – Activities where students take on specific characters or positions, requiring them to understand and represent different perspectives.

ROUND-ROBIN SHARING – A debriefing technique where each participant takes turns sharing thoughts or insights.

SCHOLAR PHASE – The academic phase (ages 12-18) that follows the Discovery Phase, encompassing Practice Scholar, Apprentice Scholar, and Self-Directed Scholar stages. Through deep engagement with great ideas, historical figures, and meaningful places, this phase not only develops academic ability but also shapes character, touches hearts, and influences families across generations.

SELF-DIRECTED SCHOLAR – The advanced Scholar Phase (typically ages 16+) characterized by independent study initiatives, research and application, and 40-80 hours of weekly study time.

SIMULATIONS – A learning environment where theory transforms into lived experience.

SIX POINTS OF EDITING – A comprehensive framework for reviewing writing that includes Target Audience, Content Relevance, Structure and Form, Flow, Punctuation and Grammar, and Readability.

SKILLS – One of the five Leadership Ladders representing specific technical competencies and "how-to" knowledge needed for tasks.

SOCRATIC DISCUSSION – A method of group dialogue that uses probing questions to encourage critical thinking and deeper understanding.

SPIRITUAL EYES – The mentor's ability to deeply perceive and understand students' needs, potential, and next steps for growth.[13]

STRUCTURE AND FORM – One of the six points of editing concerning organizational patterns and logical arrangement of ideas.

STUDENTS – The central players in Leadership Education who take active responsibility for their own learning journey and development.

SYNTOPICAL READING – The highest level of reading involving comparing and contrasting ideas across multiple texts to form new insights.[14]

TAXIS – The element of organization and structure in presentation, one of the five classical rhetorical elements.[15]

TESTING, PERFORMANCE, AND TEACHING – A learning environment where learning deepens through demonstration and sharing.

TUTORIAL – A learning environment where personalized guidance nurtures individual growth.

VISION – One of the five Leadership Ladders representing a student's understanding of why something, such as learning, matters and where it leads.

VOICE – A writer's unique style and perspective expressed through their writing.

WHOLE STORIES – Narratives that present an intact world where good and evil are clearly defined and justice prevails.[16]

WORKSHOPS – Interactive learning sessions that blend lecture content with interactive activities.

WRITING – A learning environment where thoughts and feelings clarify and personal voice emerges.

CHAPTER END NOTES

Introduction

1. Oliver DeMille, *A Thomas Jefferson Education*, 2nd ed. (Cedar City, UT: George Wythe University Press, 2009).

2. Chaim Potok, *The Chosen* (New York: Simon & Schuster, 1967).

3. Charles Dickens, *Oliver Twist* (New York: Barnes & Noble Classics, 1995).

4. "Educate," Online Etymology Dictionary, accessed February 16, 2025, https://www.etymonline.com/word/educate.

Chapter 2

1. DeMille, *A Thomas Jefferson Education*, 34.

2. Ibid., 35.

3. Oliver DeMille and Rachel DeMille, *Leadership Education: The Phases of Learning* (Springville, UT: TJEd Online, 2008), 251-266.

4. Information in this section is drawn from DeMille, *A Thomas Jefferson Education*, 34.

Chapter 3:

1. Shinichi Suzuki, *Nurtured by Love: A New Approach to Education* (New York: Exposition Press, 1969), 56-60.

2. F. Enzio Busche, Yearning for the Living God: Reflections from the Life of F. Enzio Busche, ed. Tracie A. Lamb (Salt Lake City: Deseret Book, 2004).

3. Suzuki, *Nurtured by Love*, 56-60.

4. Busche, *Yearning for the Living God*.

5. Joshua Cooper Ramo, *The Seventh Sense: Power, Fortune, and Survival in the Age of Networks* (New York: Back Bay Books/Little, Brown and Company, 2018), 303.

6. Ibid., 300.

7. Suzuki, *Nurtured by Love*, 56-60.

8. Aristotle, *Nicomachean Ethics*, trans. Roger Crisp, 2nd ed. (Cambridge: Cambridge University Press, 2014).

9. DeMille, Oliver, and Tiffany Earl. *The Student Whisperer*. TJEd Online, 2011.

10. Tiffany Earl and Aneladee Milne, "Classic Call: Language of Freedom," LEMI, February 2023, podcast, 1:18:09, https://lemiworks.com/2023/02/classic-call-language-of-freedom/ (accessed February 19, 2025).

11. Earl and Milne, "Classic Call: Scholar Ladders."

12. Angela Duckworth, *Grit: The Power of Passion and Perseverance*, First Scribner hardcover edition (New York: Scribner, 2016).

Chapter 4:

1. Suzuki, *Nurtured by Love*, 56-60..

2. Ramo, *The Seventh Sense*, 35.

3. Mortimer J. Adler, *The Great Conversation: A Reader's Guide to Great Books of the Western World*, 2nd ed. (Chicago: Encyclopaedia Britannica, 1990).

4. Wilson A. Bentley and W. J. Humphreys, *Snow Crystals* (New York: McGraw-Hill, 1931).

5. Claude-Michel Schönberg, *Les Misérables: A Musical*

(London; Milwaukee, WI: Alain Boublil Music; Exclusively distributed by H. Leonard, 1998).

6. Daniel Pink, *Drive: The Surprising Truth About What Motivates Us* (New York: Riverhead Books, 2011).

7. Aneladee Milne, *The Mentor's Handbook* (Hemet, CA: Genius Paradigm Publishing, 2025)

Chapter 5:

1. *Amy Bowler - Foundations of Leadership*, LEMIWorks!, podcast, April 2023, accessed February 16, 2025, https://lemiworks.com/2023/04/amy-bowler-foundations-of-leadership/.

2. LEMI-U.com

3. Leadership Education Mentoring Institute, *Family Foundations Membership (Not the Training)*, LEMI Homeschool, accessed February 19, 2025, https://www.lemihomeschool.com/shop/p/family-foundations-membership-not-the-training.

Chapter 6:

1. Paraphrased from Lao Tzu, Tao Te Ching, trans. Stephen Mitchell (London: Frances Lincoln Limited, 2009), chapter 17.

2. *Family Foundations Membership*, https://www.lemihomeschool.com/shop/p/family-foundations-membership-not-the-training.

3. Nicholeen Peck, *Parenting: A House United: Changing Children's Hearts and Behaviors by Teaching Self-Government* (2020).

4. *Revolutionary Families*, accessed February 19, 2025, https://revolutionaryfamilies.simplecast.com/.

5.   Carol S. Dweck, *Mindset: The New Psychology of Success* (New York: Ballantine Books, 2007).

Chapter 7:

1.   Henry David Thoreau, *Walden* (New York: E.P. Dutton & Co., Inc., 1959).

2.   Plato, *The Republic*, trans. Allan Bloom, 3rd ed. (New York: Basic Books, 2016), Book VII, 514a–520a.

3.   Shakespeare, William. *Romeo and Juliet*. Dover Thrift Editions. Mineola, NY: Dover Publications, 1993.

4.   Plato, *The Republic*, 514a–520a.

5.   Ibid., 514a–520a.

6.   Milne, *The Mentor's Handbook*.

7.   Joseph Grenny et al., *Crucial Conversations: Tools for Talking When Stakes are High*, 3rd ed. (New York: McGraw Hill, 2021).

Chapter 8:

1.   Frederick Douglass, *Narrative of the Life of Frederick Douglass* (New York: Dover Publications, 2016), 29.

2.   Ibid., 98.

3.   Owen Wister, *The Virginian* (New York: Penguin Books, 1988).

4.   Jacques Lusseyran, *And There Was Light: The Extraordinary Memoir of a Blind Hero of the French Resistance in World War II*, 3rd ed. (Novato, CA: New World Library, 2014)

5.   J.R.R. Tolkien, *The Hobbit: or, There and Back Again* (Boston: Houghton Mifflin Harcourt, 2014).

6. J.R.R. Tolkien, *The Lord of the Rings*, 2nd ed. (Boston: Houghton Mifflin Co., 1993).

7. Homer, *The Odyssey*, trans. Richmond Lattimore (New York: Harper & Row, 1967).

8. Randall E. Stross, *The Wizard of Menlo Park: How Thomas Alva Edison Invented the Modern World* (New York: Crown Publishers, 2007).

9. Daniel Tayolor, *The Healing Power of Stories: Creating Yourself Through the Stories of Your Life* (New York: Doubleday, 1996).

10. C. S. Lewis, *The Chronicles of Narnia* (New York: HarperCollins Publishers, 2001).

11. Viktor E. Frankl, *Man's Search for Meaning* (Boston: Beacon Press, 2006).

12. Harper Lee, *To Kill a Mockingbird* (New York: Grand Central Publishing, 1988).

13. Ji-Li Jiang, *Red Scarf Girl: A Memoir of the Cultural Revolution* (New York: HarperCollins, 2018).

14. Jung Chang, *Wild Swans: Three Daughters of China* (New York: Simon & Schuster, 1991).

15. C. S. Lewis, *The Chronicles of Narnia*.

16. Mortimer J. Adler and Charles Van Doren, *How to Read a Book: The Classic Guide to Intelligent Reading* (New York: Simon and Schuster, 1972).

17. Ibid., 17, 26.

18. Ibid., 18-19, 31-32.

19. Kate DiCamillo, *The Tale of Despereaux: Being the Story of a Mouse, a Princess, Some Soup, and a Spool of Thread*

(Somerville: Candlewick Press, 2003).

20. Adler and Van Doren, *How to Read a Book*, 19, 31.

21. Ibid., 108.

22. Ibid., 19-20.

23. Robert M. Hutchins, *The Great Conversation*, in Great Books of the Western World, vol. 1 (Chicago: Encyclopædia Britannica, 1952).

24. Brianna Schubert, "How to Start a Commonplace Book (And Why You Should Try It)," *The Good Trade*, accessed February 16, 2025, https://www.thegoodtrade.com/features/what-is-a-commonplace-book/.

25. William Shakespeare, *The Merchant of Venice*, ed. Peter Holland (London: Penguin Classics, 2015).

26. Ibid., Act 4 Scene 1.

27. William Shakespeare, *Romeo and Juliet*, ed. Peter Holland (London: Penguin Classics, 2015).

28. Aesop, *The Fables of Aesop*, adapted by Jean de La Fontaine and Samuel Croxall (Chicago: A. Whitman & Co., 1925).

29. Adler and Van Doren, *How to Read a Book*, 17, 26.

30. Shakespeare, *Merchant of Venice*.

31. Adler and Van Doren, *How to Read a Book*, 18-19, 31-32.

32. Shakespeare, *Romeo and Juliet*.

33. Adler and Van Doren, *How to Read a Book*, 19, 31.

34. Alexander Hamilton, James Madison, and John Jay, *The Federalist Papers*, ed. Clinton Rossiter (New York: Signet Classics, 2003).

35. Adler and Van Doren, *How to Read a Book*, 19.

36. Stross, *The Wizard of Menlo Park*.

37. Salvatore Mangione, "Was Leonardo da Vinci Dyslexic?" *The American Journal of Medicine* 132, no. 7 (July 2019): 892-893

38. Bacon, Francis. *The Essays of Francis Bacon*. London: John Murray, 1887.

39. Adler and Van Doren, *How to Read a Book*, 19.

40. Taylor, *Healing Power of Stories*

41. Brock L. Eide and Fernette F. Eide, *The Dyslexic Advantage: Unlocking the Hidden Potential of the Dyslexic Brain* (New York: Plume, 2023).

42. *LEMIWorks Podcast*, lemiworks.com.

Chapter 9

1. Corrie Ten Boom, *The Hiding Place* (Washington Depot, Conn.: Chosen Books, 1971), 167-168.

2. E. M.Forster, *Aspects of the Novel*. New York: Harcourt, Brace & Company, 1927, 151.

3. Strunk, William, and E. B. White. *The Elements of Style*. New York: Allyn and Bacon, 1979.

4. C.S. Lewis, *The Complete Works of C.S. Lewis* (Various publishers, 1919-2013).

5. Strunk and White, *The Elements of Style*.

Chapter 10

1. New College, Oxford, Study Guide For Undergraduates (Oxford, UK, 2019), 5.

Chapter 11

1. William Shakespeare, *A Midsummer Night's Dream*, ed. Barbara A. Mowat and Paul Werstine (New York: Washington Square Press, 2004).

Chapter 12

1. Jane Austen, *Pride and Prejudice* (London: Penguin Books, 2014), 62.

2. Aristotle, *Rhetoric*, trans. W. Rhys Roberts, Book 1, Part 2, accessed February 16, 2025, http://classics.mit.edu/Aristotle/rhetoric.1.i.html.

3. Ibid., Book II.

4. Ibid., Book I, Part 2.

5. Ibid., Book III, Chapter 13.

6. Ibid.,, Book III, Chapter 5.

Chapter 13

1. Tatiana Fallon, Simulations Book, Leadership Education Mentoring Institute, accessed February 19, 2025, https://www.lemihomeschool.com/shop

Chapter 14

1. DeMille, A Thomas Jefferson Education, 22.

Chapter 15

1. Milne, The Mentor's Handbook.

Chapter 16

1. Thomas Paine, Common Sense (Philadelphia: W. and T. Bradford, 1776)

Glossary

1. Adler and Van Doren, *How to Read a Book*, 19, 31.

2. Taylor, *The Healing Power of Stories*.

3. Ibid.

4. DeMille, *A Thomas Jefferson Education*, 22.

5. Educate, *Online Etymology Dictionary*.

6. Adler and Van Doren, *How to Read a Book*, 17.

7. Aristotle, *Rhetoric*, Book 1, Part 2.

8. Dweck, Mindset.

9. Taylor, *The Healing Power of Stories*.

10. Adler and Van Doren, *How to Read a Book*, 18-19.

11. Aristotle, *Rhetoric*, Book III, Chapter 5.

12. Ibid., Book II.

13. Suzuki, *Nurtured by Love*, 56-60

14. Adler and Van Doren, *How to Read a Book*, 19-20.

15. Aristotle, Rhetoric, Book III, Chapter 13.

16. Taylor, *The Healing Power of Stories*.

31420456R00186